# Old Testament
# Introduction

 BIBLIOGRAPHIES

**Tremper Longman III**
General Editor and Old Testament Editor

**Craig A. Evans**
New Testament Editor

1. Pentateuch
2. Historical Books
3. Poetry and Wisdom
4. Prophecy and Apocalyptic
5. Jesus
6. Synoptic Gospels
7. Johannine Writings
8. Luke–Acts
9. Pauline Writings
10. Hebrews and General Epistles
11. Old Testament Introduction
12. New Testament Introduction
13. Old Testament Theology
14. New Testament Theology

BIBLIOGRAPHIES No. 11

# Old Testament Introduction

Edwin C. Hostetter

Baker Books
A Division of Baker Book House Co
Grand Rapids, Michigan 49516

Published by Baker Books
a division of Baker Book House Company
P.O. Box 6287, Grand Rapids, MI 49516-6287

Printed in the United States of America

### Library of Congress Cataloging-in-Publication Data

Hostetter, Edwin C., 1957–
    Old Testament introduction / Edwin C. Hostetter.
        p.    cm. — (IBR bibliographies ; no. 11)
    Contents: Criticism — Ancient texts and versions — Language —
Cognate literature — The environment.
    ISBN-8010-2017-4 (pbk.)
    1. Bible. O.T.—Introductions—Bibliography. I. Title. II. Series.
Z7772.A1H67      1995
[BS1140.2]
016.2216'1—dc20           95-8768

# Contents

# Series Preface

With the proliferation of journals and publishing houses dedicated to biblical studies, it has become impossible for even the most dedicated scholar to keep in touch with the vast materials now available for research in all the different parts of the canon. How much more difficult for the minister, rabbi, student, or interested layperson! Herein lies the importance of bibliographies and in particular this series—IBR Bibliographies.

Bibliographies help guide students to works relevant to their research interests. They cut down the time needed to locate materials, thus providing the researcher with more time to read, assimilate, and write. These benefits are especially true for the IBR Bibliographies. First, the series is conveniently laid out along the major divisions of the canon, with four volumes planned on the Old Testament, six on the New Testament, and four on methodology (see page 2). Each volume will contain approximately five hundred entries, arranged under various topics to allow for ease of reference. Since the possible entries far exceed this number, the compiler of each volume must select the more important and helpful works for inclusion. Furthermore, the entries are briefly annotated in order to inform the reader about their contents more specifically, once again giving guidance to the appropriate material and saving time by preventing the all too typical "wild goose chase" in the library.

One of the problems with published bibliographies in the past is that they are soon out of date. The development of computer-based publishing has changed this, however, and it is the plan of the Institute for Biblical Research and Baker Book House to publish updates of each volume about every five years.

Since the series is designed primarily for American and British students, the emphasis is on works written in English, with a five-percent limit on titles not translated into English. Fortunately, a number of the most important foreign-language works have been translated into English, and wherever this is the case this information is included along with the original publication data. Again keeping in mind the needs of the student, we have decided to list the English translation before the original title (for chronological purposes, the titles are arranged according to the dates of their original publication).

These bibliographies are presented under the sponsorship of the Institute for Biblical Research (IBR), an organization of evangelical Christian scholars with specialties in both Old and New Testaments and their ancillary disciplines. The IBR has met annually since 1970; its name and constitution were adopted in 1973. Besides its annual meetings (normally held the evening and morning prior to the annual meeting of the Society of Biblical Literature), the institute publishes a journal, *Bulletin for Biblical Research*, and conducts regional study groups on various biblical themes in several areas of the United States and Canada. The Institute for Biblical Research encourages and fosters scholarly research among its members, all of whom are at a level to qualify for a university lectureship. Finally, the IBR and the series editor extend their thanks to Baker Book House for its efforts to bring this series to publication. In particular, we would like to thank David Aiken for his wise guidance in giving shape to the project.

Tremper Longman III
Westminster Theological Seminary

# 1

# Criticism

## 1.1 General Introductions

The books listed here deal with such background issues as authorship, date, purpose, and so forth, related to the writings of the Old Testament/Hebrew Bible. Included in this section are scholarly works, which tend to bear the name "introduction" in the title, and several surveys more popular in nature. Some of the volumes handle deuterocanonical Scripture in addition to protocanonical Scripture, while a few treat the apocrypha alone.

1    R. B. Dillard and T. Longman III. *Old Testament Introduction*. Grand Rapids: Zondervan, 1994.

Covering historical background, literary analysis, and theological interpretation, this volume gives readers information necessary to understand the Hebrew Bible according to its original intention.

2    A. R. Ceresko. *Introduction to the Old Testament: A Liberation Perspective*. Maryknoll, N.Y.: Orbis/London: Chapman, 1992.

The author uses a sociopolitical approach to introduce students to the Old Testament. The book features discussion questions, bibliographical notes, and many maps and illustrations.

3    P. R. House. *Old Testament Survey*. Nashville: Broadman, 1992.

The author tries to help beginning students understand the major developments of the Old Testament books. He follows the canonical order of the Masoretic Text.

4    M. Duggan. *The Consuming Fire: A Christian Introduction to the Old Testament*. San Francisco: Ignatius, 1991.

While covering standard issues, this comprehensive guidebook also describes the manner in which the Old Testament (including the deuterocanonical/apocryphal writings) reaches fulfillment in Christ—according to the perspective of the New Testament.

5    A. E. Hill and J. H. Walton. *A Survey of the Old Testament*. Grand Rapids: Zondervan, 1991.

The authors attempt to balance the literary, historical, and theological issues pertaining to the Old Testament as a whole and to each individual book.

6    R. J. Coggins. *Introducing the Old Testament*. Oxford Bible Series. Oxford: Oxford University, 1990.

This study—which considers the importance of sociology and anthropology, liberationist and feminist perspectives, and literary criticism—eruditely leads those who come to the Old Testament for the first time.

7    W. L. Humphreys. *Crisis and Story: Introduction to the Old Testament*. 2d ed. Mountain View: Mayfield, 1990.

The writer seeks to show that stories about Israel arose at major crises or turning points in its life. This introduction follows a historical order of the literary production of the Old Testament books.

8    S. J. Schultz. *The Old Testament Speaks*. 4th ed. San Francisco: Harper, 1990.

The author utilizes a comparative approach and demonstrates an acquaintance with insights from archaeological and epigraphic finds in the Near East.

9    J. A. Soggin. *Introduction to the Old Testament*. 3d ed. Translated by J. Bowden. Louisville: Westminster/London:

SCM, 1989. Original title: *Introduzione all'Antico Testamento*. Brescia: Paideia, 1987.

This enlightened introduction includes an analysis of the apocryphal/deuterocanonical books. A pair of appendixes examine pre-Hellenistic inscriptions from Palestine and Elephantine.

**10** J. Carmody, D. L. Carmody, and R. J. Cohn. *Exploring the Hebrew Bible*. Englewood Cliffs, N.J.: Prentice, 1988.

In this comprehensive treatment at a beginning level, the authors include for each book of the Old Testament a section entitled "lasting significance" that places the wisdom of the Bible in broader context.

**11** H. J. Flanders, R. W. Crapps, and D. A. Smith. *People of the Covenant: An Introduction to the Old Testament*. 3d ed. New York: Oxford University, 1988.

This introduction contains excellent maps and illustrations, and it reflects theological as well as literary discernment and sensitivity.

**12** A. L. Laffey. *An Introduction to the Old Testament: A Feminist Perspective*. Philadelphia: Fortress, 1988. British edition: *Wives, Harlots and Concubines: The Old Testament in Feminist Perspective*. London: SPCK, 1990.

This endeavor, which is intended to serve as a supplement to traditional introductions, surveys the Old Testament with an eye for stories and issues that concern women.

**13** J. Drane. *Introducing the Old Testament*. San Francisco: Harper/Tring; England: Lion/Sutherland; Australia: Albatross, 1987.

The richly illustrated text explores the writings and beliefs of the Hebrew nation in the context of their historical and cultural background.

**14** H. L. Willmington. *Willmington's Survey of the Old Testament: An Overview of the Scriptures from Creation to Christ*. Wheaton: Victor, 1987.

By treating the Old Testament books when arranged chronologically, the author hopes to show how God revealed truth progressively. Every lesson comprises basic information, application, and illustration.

**15**   B. W. Anderson. *Understanding the Old Testament.* 4th ed. Englewood Cliffs, N.J.: Prentice, 1986. British edition: *The Living World of the Old Testament.* 4th ed. Harlow: Longman, 1988.

This college-level survey of the Old Testament highlights the history and religion of Israel. The author uses archaeological data and modern secondary literature well.

**16**   P. C. Craigie. *The Old Testament: Its Background, Growth, and Content.* Nashville: Abingdon/Burlington: Welch, 1986.

The writer surveys the books of the Old Testament as in a standard introduction but also provides a brief history of ancient Israel.

**17**   J. L. Crenshaw. *Story and Faith: A Guide to the Old Testament.* New York: Macmillan, 1986. Reprinted *Old Testament Story and Faith: A Literary and Theological Introduction.* Peabody: Hendrickson, 1992.

The author regards archaeology, history, and sociology as secondary to the task of recovering the artistry and craft behind the biblical text. Students become exposed to the vocabulary, stories, and imagery of the Hebrew Bible and of the Greek Old Testament's apocrypha/deuterocanonicals.

**18**   N. K. Gottwald. *The Hebrew Bible: A Socio-Literary Introduction.* Philadelphia: Fortress, 1985.

The writer applies his sociological approach (along with literary insights) in an introductory study of the Hebrew Bible.

**19**   R. Rendtorff. *The Old Testament: An Introduction.* Translated by J. Bowden. Philadelphia: Fortress/London: SCM, 1985. Original title: *Das Alte Testament.* Neukirchen-Vluyn, Germany: Neukirchener, 1983.

The writer merges his interests regarding the history, institutions, and literature of the Old Testament into a single volume.

**20** L. Boadt. *Reading the Old Testament: An Introduction.*
New York: Paulist, 1984.

This is a solid, popular work of a high standard, with a
conscientious approach to the texts.

**21** W. H. Schmidt. *Old Testament Introduction.* Translated by
M. J. O'Connell. New York: Crossroad, 1984. British edition: *Introduction to the Old Testament.* London: SCM,
1984. Original title: *Einführung in das Alte Testament.* Berlin: de Gruyter, 1979.

Written by a well-known Old Testament interpreter, this
is an excellent volume—even though limited to the
books of the Hebrew canon.

**22** J. M. Efird. *The Old Testament Writings: History, Literature, and Interpretation.* Atlanta: Knox, 1982.

The author handily and nontechnically presents main-
line, critical Old Testament scholarship up to about the
middle of the twentieth century.

**23** W. S. LaSor, D. A. Hubbard, and F. W. Bush. *Old Testament
Survey: The Message, Form, and Background of the Old
Testament.* Grand Rapids: Eerdmans, 1982.

The authors have interacted with recent scholarship and
produced an eminently readable volume appropriate for
seminary classrooms.

**24** B. S. Childs. *Introduction to the Old Testament as Scripture.* Philadelphia: Fortress/London: SCM, 1979.

To the historical-critical method of interpretation, the
author adds a consideration of the Old Testament books
as part of the Christian canon. Consequently, this introduction contains a great deal of theology.

**25** J. H. Hayes. *An Introduction to Old Testament Study.*
Nashville: Abingdon, 1979.

While not pretending to be a full-scale introduction, this
well-organized and lucidly written work describes the development of the Old Testament and examines its main
sections for beginning students.

**26**   H. D. Hummel. *The Word Becoming Flesh: An Introduction to the Origin, Purpose, and Meaning of the Old Testament*. St. Louis: Concordia, 1979.

This volume, which highlights theological questions, studies the history and organization as well as the interpreters and critics of the Old Testament.

**27**   I. L. Jensen. *Jensen's Survey of the Old Testament: Search and Discover*. Chicago: Moody, 1978.

This survey provides practical guidance for reading the Old Testament and offers helpful insight into the geographical and historical context of its development.

**28**   N. L. Geisler. *A Popular Survey of the Old Testament*. Grand Rapids: Baker, 1977.

Illustrated with charts, maps, and photographs, and written in an informal style, this Christ-centered survey discusses the themes of the various groups of Old Testament books.

**29**   L. Rost. *Judaism outside the Hebrew Canon: An Introduction to the Documents*. Translated by D. E. Green. Nashville: Abingdon, 1976. Original title: *Einleitung in die alttestamentlichen Apokryphen und Pseudepigraphen*. Heidelberg: Quelle, 1971.

This authoritative resource treats the historicity, literary genre, authorship, and religious meaning of Old Testament apocrypha, pseudepigrapha, and major Qumran texts.

**30**   O. Kaiser. *Introduction to the Old Testament: A Presentation of Its Results and Problems*. Translated by J. Sturdy. Minneapolis: Augsburg/Oxford: Blackwell, 1975. Original title: *Einleitung in das Alte Testament*. Gütersloh: Mohn, 1975.

This short, readable work is designed for students, teachers, and pastors as an introduction to the books of the Hebrew canon of the Old Testament.

**31**   G. L. Archer, Jr. *A Survey of Old Testament Introduction*. Rev. ed. Chicago: Moody, 1974.

Although the writer provides a careful study of the books of the Old Testament, he has adopted a rather apologetic and polemical perspective.

**32** J. G. Williams. *Understanding the Old Testament.* New York: Barron's, 1972.

The author explains the central ideas and motifs of each Old Testament book in a scholarly yet easily understandable manner.

**33** R. K. Harrison. *Introduction to the Old Testament.* Grand Rapids: Eerdmans, 1969; London: Tyndale, 1970.

Besides a book-by-book analysis of the Old Testament (including the apocrypha/deuterocanonicals), the author presents a mass of information on archaeology, textual criticism, history, and religion. This admirable reference tool reflects a stance respectful of Scripture.

**34** G. Fohrer. *Introduction to the Old Testament.* Translated by D. Green. Nashville: Abingdon/London: SPCK, 1968. Original title: *Einleitung in das Alte Testament.* Heidelberg: Quelle, 1965.

The author espouses a coordinated use of form-critical, traditio-historical, and literary-critical methods in approaching the biblical writings. This comprehensive, technical introduction is nonetheless limited to the books of the Masoretic Text.

**35** H. H. Rowley. *The Growth of the Old Testament.* 3d ed. London: Hutchinson, 1967.

The author presents a concise and readable account of how the Old Testament came into being and received the shape in which we have it today.

**36** O. Eissfeldt. *The Old Testament: An Introduction.* Translated by P. R. Ackroyd. New York: Harper/Oxford: Blackwell, 1965. Original title: *Einleitung in das Alte Testament.* Tübingen: Mohr, 1964.

The author begins with the preliterary materials of the Old Testament and ends with the transmission and translation of the text. In between, this classic isagogical resource discusses in detail every biblical book as well as the apocrypha, pseudepigrapha, and similar Qumran writings.

**37**   S. Sandmel. *The Hebrew Scriptures: An Introduction to Their Literature and Religious Ideas.* New York: Knopf, 1963. Reprinted New York: Oxford University, 1978.

This prominent Jewish-American scholar aims his non-technical introduction of basic material at the beginner.

**38**   J. A. Bewer. *The Literature of the Old Testament.* Revised by E. G. Kraeling. 3d ed. Records of Civilization: Sources and Studies 5. New York: Columbia University, 1962.

This introduction is technical and critical in character at the same time that it displays a confessional stance.

**39**   L. H. Brockington. *A Critical Introduction to the Apocrypha.* Studies in Theology. London: Duckworth, 1961.

The writer brackets discussion of the separate apocryphal/deuterocanonical books of the Old Testament with a historical survey of the period to which they belong and an explanation of their merit and worth.

**40**   A. Weiser. *The Old Testament: Its Formation and Development.* Translated by D. M. Barton. New York: Association, 1961. British edition: *Introduction to the Old Testament.* London: Darton, 1961. Original title: *Einleitung in das Alte Testament.* Göttingen: Vandenhoeck, 1963.

The author takes into account the theological value of the material he examines. He includes sections on the apocryphal/deuterocanonical works as well as certain pseudepigraphal ones.

**41**   E. J. Young. *An Introduction to the Old Testament.* Rev. ed. Grand Rapids: Eerdmans/London: Tyndale, 1960.

Written in a winsome style, this brief study of Old Testament isagogics is incisive and well informed.

**42**   G. W. Anderson. *A Critical Introduction to the Old Testament.* Studies in Theology. London: Duckworth, 1959.

This manual assesses important theories about the nature and composition of the Old Testament books and describes the structure and contents of the several books.

**43**  B. M. Metzger. *An Introduction to the Apocrypha*. New York: Oxford University, 1957.

> The author supplies a scholarly analysis of the individual books of the Old Testament apocrypha before probing the use of the apocrypha/deuterocanonicals within Christianity and their influence on the arts.

**44**  A. Bentzen. *Introduction to the Old Testament*. 2d ed. Copenhagen: Gad, 1952.

> This work offers a particularly valuable guide to the questions and methods of the Scandinavian school of biblical study. The volume includes the apocryphal/deuterocanonical books of the Old Testament.

**45**  M. F. Unger. *Introductory Guide to the Old Testament*. Grand Rapids: Zondervan, 1951.

> The writer, who views Scripture as the Word of God and as an intimate part of history, cautiously analyzes critical hypotheses.

## 1.2 Specific Methods

This section describes the wide variety of critical ways used to explicate the Old Testament/Hebrew Bible. Typical categories are literary, form, canonical, anthropological/sociological, and tradition criticism. Works cover narrative and poetry, single or multiple methods, and even discussion of the canon per se.

**46**  H.-J. Tertel. *Text and Transmission: An Empirical Model for the Literary Development of Old Testament Narratives*. Beihefte zur Zeitschrift für die alttestamentliche Wissenschaft 221. Berlin: de Gruyter, 1994.

> This study ascertains criteria for evaluating primary and secondary historiography in scriptural narratives by means of the successive editions of Assyrian royal annals.

**47**  W. G. E. Watson. *Traditional Techniques in Classical Hebrew Poetry*. JSOTSup. 170. Sheffield: JSOT, 1994.

> After an opening survey of current work on Biblical Hebrew verse, this welcome anthology covers topics ranging widely from parallelism to ethnopoetics.

**48**  J. C. Exum and D. J. A. Clines (eds.). *The New Literary Criticism and the Hebrew Bible*. Sheffield: JSOT, 1993. Valley Forge: Trinity, 1994.

In essays by leading international Hebrew Bible scholars, the methods and practice of reader response criticism and deconstruction, as well as feminist, materialist, and psychoanalytic approaches, are represented here.

**49**  D. M. Gunn and D. N. Fewell. *Narrative in the Hebrew Bible*. The Oxford Bible Series. Oxford: Oxford University, 1993.

Attempting to be both theoretical and practical, the authors combine discussion of methods and the business of reading in general with numerous illustrations through readings of particular texts.

**50**  S. R. Haynes and S. L. McKenzie (eds.). *To Each Its Own Meaning: An Introduction to Biblical Criticisms and Their Application*. Louisville: Westminster/London: Chapman, 1993.

This single volume impressively introduces the reader to the most important methods of Old and New Testament criticism by giving equal time to historical and literary approaches.

**51**  S. Niditch. *Folklore and the Hebrew Bible*. Guides to Biblical Scholarship. Minneapolis: Fortress, 1993.

This helpful textbook first brings the student into conversation with contemporary folklorists and then applies their methodologies to a range of exemplary passages.

**52**  R. C. Culley. *Themes and Variations: A Study of Action in Biblical Narrative*. Semeia Studies. Atlanta: Scholars, 1992.

This clearly written study identifies and illustrates repeated yet variable patterns in the stories of the Hebrew Bible, especially patterns of action.

**53**  P. R. House (ed.). *Beyond Form Criticism: Essays in Old Testament Literary Criticism*. Sources for Biblical and Theological Study 2. Winona Lake, Ind.: Eisenbrauns, 1992.

Ideal for classroom use, this work fills a significant void by providing a comprehensive introduction to the rapidly expanding field of Old Testament literary criticism.

**54**   D. L. Petersen and K. H. Richards. *Interpreting Hebrew Poetry*. Guides to Biblical Scholarship. Minneapolis: Fortress, 1992.

> The writers offer an authoritative guide to recent discussion about parallelism, meter, rhythm, and other distinctive aspects of the one-third of the Hebrew Bible that is in poetic form.

**55**   M. G. Brett. *Biblical Criticism in Crisis? The Impact of the Canonical Approach on Old Testament Studies*. Cambridge: Cambridge University, 1991.

> The writer contends that the canonical approach to Old Testament study makes a distinctive contribution without displacing other traditions of historical, social scientific, or literary inquiry.

**56**   S. Z. Leiman. *The Canonization of Hebrew Scripture: The Talmudic and Midrashic Evidence*. 2d ed. Transactions of the Connecticut Academy of Arts and Sciences 47. New Haven: Connecticut Academy of Arts and Sciences, 1991.

> A most original analysis of the Talmudic and Midrashic materials, this key book departs from the older view that Jamnia/Jabneh was the locus of canonization.

**57**   J. P. Rosenblatt and J. C. Sitterson, Jr. (eds.). *"Not in Heaven": Coherence and Complexity in Biblical Narrative*. Indiana Studies in Biblical Literature. Bloomington: Indiana University, 1991.

> The Old Testament is pluralized, deified, and assaulted by the contributors (Jews, Christians, and neither) to this volume—a brilliant demonstration of what clever readers can do with texts.

**58**   J. L. Ska. *"Our Fathers Have Told Us": Introduction to the Analysis of Hebrew Narratives*. Subsidia Biblica 13. Rome: Biblical Institute, 1990.

> The author introduces beginners to the various concepts of Old Testament narrative analysis, explaining how scholars in the field apply their tools to concrete cases.

**59**   R. Vasholz. *The Old Testament Canon in the Old Testament Church: The Internal Rationale for Old Testament*

*Canonicity.* Ancient Near Eastern Texts and Studies 7. Lewiston, N.Y.: Mellen, 1990.

Both sophisticated and imaginative, the author's style will permit not just specialists but any serious investigator (like a pastor) to benefit from immediate perusal and future reference.

**60**   S. Bar-Efrat. *Narrative Art in the Bible.* Translated by D. Shefer-Vanson. Bible and Literature Series 17. Sheffield: Almond, 1989. Original title: *The Art of the Biblical Story* (in Hebrew). Tel-Aviv: Sifriat Poalim, 1984.

The author systematically describes and lavishly illustrates a way of reading that is based on the employment of tools and principles current in the study of literature.

**61**   L. A. Schökel. *A Manual of Hebrew Poetics.* Subsidia Biblica 11. Rome: Biblical Institute, 1988.

Initiating the reader into the stylistic treatment of poetry, the author discusses techniques like sonority, rhythm, imagery, dialogue, composition, and figures of speech.

**62**   W. van der Meer and J. C. de Moor (eds.). *The Structural Analysis of Biblical and Canaanite Poetry.* JSOTSup 74. Sheffield: JSOT, 1988.

This introduction to a new method of structural examination of ancient poetry incorporates studies ranging from Ugarit to the New Testament, although the main emphasis is on the Old Testament.

**63**   D. Damrosch. *The Narrative Covenant: Transformations of Genre in the Growth of Biblical Literature.* San Francisco: Harper, 1987. Reprinted Ithaca: Cornell University, 1991.

Integrating the fields of comparative, text-historical, and literary study, this project has applied structural and genre analysis to the historical problem of the development of Old Testament narrative.

**64**   P. G. Kirkpatrick. *The Old Testament and Folklore Study.* JSOTSup 62. Sheffield: JSOT, 1987.

This interdisciplinary volume explores the implications of contemporary folklore research for present-day theories about the composition and transmission of the patriarchal narratives.

**65**   J. A. Sanders. *From Sacred Story to Sacred Text: Canon as Paradigm*. Philadelphia: Fortress, 1987.

The essays in this book on canonical criticism address students, pastors, and lay people and stress the full historical process whereby the canon grew, developed, and was shaped.

**66**   W. G. E. Watson. *Classical Hebrew Poetry: A Guide to Its Techniques*. 2d ed. JSOTSup 26. Sheffield: JSOT, 1986.

This book—comprising general theory and worked examples—gives an account of the methods and results of current scholarship and provides both lecturers and students with guidelines for further study.

**67**   R. Alter. *The Art of Biblical Poetry*. New York: Basic, 1985.

After defining for the layperson the workings of the formal system of Old Testament poetry, this book applies them to major poetic texts.

**68**   R. Beckwith. *The Old Testament Canon of the New Testament Church and Its Background in Early Judaism*. Grand Rapids: Eerdmans/London: SPCK, 1985.

The purpose of this major contribution is to describe the canon as it existed in the first century A.D.—particularly the canon that Jesus used.

**69**   A. Berlin. *The Dynamics of Biblical Parallelism*. Bloomington: Indiana University, 1985.

Making use of linguistics in its broadest sense, the writer has attempted to get at the basics of what parallelism in the Old Testament is and how it works.

**70**   G. W. Coats (ed.). *Saga, Legend, Tale, Novella, Fable: Narrative Forms in Old Testament Literature*. JSOTSup 35. Sheffield: JSOT, 1985.

The essays in this collection present theoretical definitions for the five narrative genres listed in the title and then demonstrate the value of those definitions for exegesis of particular texts.

**71**   B. Lang (ed.). *Anthropological Approaches to the Old Testament*. Issues in Religion and Theology 8. Philadelphia: Fortress/London: SPCK, 1985.

The essays in this volume reflect biblical research done
by professional anthropologists and, to a lesser extent, research by biblical scholars engaged in anthropological
study.

**72** A. Ohler. *Studying the Old Testament from Tradition to
Canon.* Translated by D. Cairns. Edinburgh: Clark, 1985.
Original title: *Gattungen im AT.* Düsseldorf: Patmos, 1972–
73.

The structure of this book's inquiry leads from small literary units to great ones: from the single word and sentence to the question of the unity of the whole Hebrew Bible.

**73** M. Sternberg. *The Poetics of Biblical Narrative: Ideological
Literature and the Drama of Reading.* Indiana Literary Biblical Series. Bloomington: Indiana University, 1985.

The writer emphasizes not just narrative as distinct from
other genres but also those narrative principles crucial to
the marriage of ideology and a reading that governs Old
Testament poetics.

**74** J. H. Tigay (ed.). *Empirical Models for Biblical Criticism.*
Philadelphia: University of Pennsylvania, 1985.

By means of case studies, this volume illustrates the kind
of research that is involved in the documentary hypothe-
sis approach and in related critical theories.

**75** K. Jeppesen and B. Otzen (eds.). *The Productions of Time:
Tradition History in Old Testament Scholarship.* Sheffield:
Almond, 1984.

These essays on the Pentateuch, the Deuteronomistic
History, the Latter Prophets, and the Psalms deal with
traditio-historical criticism in its Scandinavian dress
from a variety of vantage points.

**76** J. A. Sanders. *Canon and Community: A Guide to Canonical Criticism.* Guides to Biblical Scholarship. Philadelphia:
Fortress, 1984.

This guide begins by explaining how and why canonical
criticism arose, and ends by outlining some of the tasks
yet to be addressed by the method.

**77** R. R. Wilson. *Sociological Approaches to the Old Testament*. Guides to Biblical Scholarship. Philadelphia: Fortress, 1984.

> This overview discusses the role of sociology in biblical interpretation and demonstrates how anthropological material might be employed to investigate Israelite history, literature, and religion.

**78** C. E. Armerding. *The Old Testament and Criticism*. Grand Rapids: Eerdmans, 1983.

> Operating from a view of Scripture as the Word of God, the author discusses the various methodological approaches that are reflected in books on Old Testament isagogics.

**79** J. Barr. *Holy Scripture: Canon, Authority, Criticism*. Philadelphia: Westminster/Oxford: Clarendon, 1983.

> The author takes up questions pertinent to such matters as biblical authority, the concept of canon, the final shape of the text, and canonical criticism.

**80** A. Berlin. *Poetics and Interpretation of Biblical Narrative*. Bible and Literature Series 9. Sheffield: Almond, 1983. Reprinted Winona Lake, Ind.: Eisenbrauns, 1994.

> This clear and cogent book for both specialists and non-specialists offers fundamental guidelines for the sensitive reading and understanding of Old Testament stories.

**81** P. D. Miscall. *The Workings of Old Testament Narrative*. Semeia Studies. Chico, Calif.: Scholars, 1983.

> Employing a literary approach that is influenced by structuralism, the author endeavors to explain why the Old Testament narratives can sustain so many different and competing interpretations.

**82** D. J. Clines, D. M. Gunn, and A. J. Hauser (eds.). *Art and Meaning: Rhetoric in Biblical Literature*. JSOTSup 19. Sheffield: JSOT, 1982.

> After an opening chapter on the rhetorical-critical method, nine chapters exhibit samples of this approach from the Old Testament (besides a pair from the New).

**83**   C. R. Fontaine. *Traditional Sayings in the Old Testament: A Contextual Study.* Bible and Literature Series 5. Sheffield: Almond, 1982.

This study analyzes the form, style, content, and contextual use of a representative number of traditional sayings that occur in the Hebrew Bible outside the corpus of wisdom literature.

**84**   R. Alter. *The Art of Biblical Narrative.* New York: Basic/London: Allen, 1981.

In a stimulating manner, the writer tries to show that the literary effects often achieved in the Old Testament were the results of art and not of artlessness.

**85**   W. W. Hallo (ed.). Scripture in Context. 4 vols. Lewiston, N.Y.: Mellen, 1980–91.

These volumes center around the comparative approach to studying biblical culture, history, or literature. Such a method analyzes the Old Testament against the background of the larger Near East.

**86**   M. O'Connor. *Hebrew Verse Structure.* Winona Lake, Ind.: Eisenbrauns, 1980.

The heart of this tome presents the major features of Old Testament verse, especially the shape and structure of the line in addition to word-, line-, and passage-level tropes.

**87**   M. J. Buss (ed.). *Encounter with the Text: Form and History in the Hebrew Bible.* Philadelphia: Fortress, 1979.

In this volume, eleven scriptural scholars show how such fields as literary criticism and the social sciences are modifying traditional approaches to form and history in the Old Testament.

**88**   J. W. Rogerson. *Anthropology and the Old Testament.* Growing Points in Theology. Oxford: Blackwell, 1978. Atlanta: Knox, 1979. Reprinted Sheffield: JSOT, 1984.

Six admirable essays survey the way in which Hebrew Bible scholars have taken up ideas and theories that have originated in modern social anthropology.

**89** R. M. Polzin. *Biblical Structuralism: Method and Subjectivity in the Study of Ancient Texts.* Semeia Supplements. Philadelphia: Fortress, 1977.

Describing how structuralism is an imaginative approach, not a distinctive methodology, the author compares and contrasts structuralism with classic samples of source criticism, form criticism, and tradition history.

**90** D. Robertson. *The Old Testament and the Literary Critic.* Guides to Biblical Scholarship. Philadelphia: Fortress, 1977.

With examples of the method applied, this book describes the process of examining parts of the Bible in order to gain an appreciation for them as literary compositions.

**91** R. C. Culley. *Studies in the Structure of Hebrew Narrative.* Semeia Supplements. Philadelphia: Fortress, 1976.

This is a very fine, short book (filled with helpful examples) for comprehending how passages are put together from their constituent elements and how that impacts exegesis.

**92** W. R. Watters. *Formula Criticism and the Poetry of the Old Testament.* Beihefte zur Zeitschrift für die alttestamentliche Wissenschaft 138. Berlin: de Gruyter, 1976.

Aiming first to explain the origins of what is called formula criticism, the author seeks second to evaluate its central theories on the basis of results from his own studies.

**93** D. A. Knight. *Rediscovering the Traditions of Israel: The Development of the Traditio-Historical Research of the Old Testament.* Rev. ed. Dissertation Series 9. Missoula, Mont.: Scholars, 1975.

This is a fine introduction to the somewhat theoretical study of the history of oral traditions as they functioned in ancient Israel before formalization in writing.

**94** E. Krentz. *The Historical-Critical Method.* Philadelphia: Fortress/London: SPCK, 1975.

This lucid volume traces the rise of historical criticism, examines its aims, methods, and presuppositions, and considers the implications of such work for theology.

**95**   J. H. Hayes (ed.). *Old Testament Form Criticism.* Trinity University Monograph Series in Religion 2. San Antonio: Trinity University, 1974.

For an understanding of the goals and presuppositions of form criticism, as well as its application in various Old Testament passages, one may consult this summary of the problem.

**96**   S. Gevirtz. *Patterns in the Early Poetry of Israel.* 2d ed. Studies in Ancient Oriental Civilization 32. Chicago: University of Chicago, 1973.

With hundreds of easy-to-follow examples, this volume on types of poetic parallelism introduces plainly how "fixed pairs" of words function in biblical poems.

**97**   W. E. Rast. *Tradition History and the Old Testament.* Guides to Biblical Scholarship. Philadelphia: Fortress, 1972.

The author offers a clear presentation of the basic principles and techniques of the traditio-historical method, comparing it with other approaches such as textual or source criticism.

**98**   J. A. Sanders. *Torah and Canon.* Philadelphia: Fortress, 1972.

Accessible to the general reader as well as the advanced student, this provocative and penetrating inquiry discusses the formation, structure, and utilization of the Old Testament as canon.

**99**   N. C. Habel. *Literary Criticism of the Old Testament.* Guides to Biblical Scholarship. Philadelphia: Fortress, 1971.

This book briefly outlines the history of Old Testament literary criticism and surveys the major techniques involved in the method, then proceeds with concrete applications.

**100**   G. M. Tucker. *Form Criticism of the Old Testament.* Guides to Biblical Scholarship. Philadelphia: Fortress, 1971.

Using samples from our own speech patterns, the author illustrates how we can recognize sundry genres of biblical literature, for instance: narrative, poetry, proverbs, ceremonies.

**101** K. Koch. *The Growth of the Biblical Tradition: The Form-Critical Method.* Translated by S. M. Cupitt. New York: Scribner's/London: Black, 1969. Original title: *Was ist Formgeschichte?* Neukirchen-Vluyn, Germany: Neukirchener, 1967.

This classic guide for beginners in theology introduces form-critical research, ponders problems of the method, and applies the approach to many Old Testament passages.

**102** R. C. Culley. *Oral Formulaic Language in the Biblical Psalms.* Near and Middle East Series 4. Toronto: University of Toronto, 1967.

This fine book examines writings from the Hebrew Bible for evidence of oral formulaic composition and explains the exegetical implications of formula criticism.

**103** C. Westermann. *Basic Forms of Prophetic Speech.* Translated by H. C. White. Philadelphia: Westminster/London: Lutterworth, 1967. Original title: *Grundformen prophetischer Rede.* Munich: Kaiser, 1964.

The writer mainly gives a form analysis of the most characteristic of the prophetic genres—the judgment speech, consisting of an accusation and an announcement.

**104** I. H. Eybers. "Historical Evidence on the Canon of the Old Testament with Special Reference to the Qumran Sect." Ph.D. diss., Duke University, 1965.

This dissertation's purpose was mainly to use the new and relevant data from manuscript discoveries at Qumran to supplement existing evidence for the delimitation of the canon's extent.

**105** A. C. Sundberg, Jr. *The Old Testament of the Early Church.* Harvard Theological Studies 20. Cambridge: Harvard University, 1964. Reprinted New York: Kraus, 1969.

This significant work has aimed to answer what the form of the Jewish canon was at the time the Christian Church arose and became separated from Judaism.

**106** E. Nielsen. *Oral Tradition: A Modern Problem in Old Testament Introduction.* Studies in Biblical Theology 11. Chicago: Allenson/London: SCM, 1954.

This succinct work, which gathers together three published articles with some additional material, introduces the modern problem of oral tradition and analyzes several traditions in the Hebrew Bible.

**107** G. Östborn. *Cult and Canon: A Study in the Canonization of the Old Testament.* Uppsala Universitets Årsskrift 1950:10. Uppsala: Lundequistska, 1950.

This investigation intends to elucidate the principal motive for selecting canonical books: namely, that the actualization in worship of Yahweh's activity exercised decisive influence on the canon's development.

# 2

# Ancient Texts and Versions

## 2.1 Editions

Here one will find printed as well as facsimile editions of the Masoretic Text, the Septuagint, the Samaritan Pentateuch, and scriptural texts discovered among the Dead Sea Scrolls. The section also records books that provide English translations of the Targums, the Peshitta, and the Vulgate.

**108** P. Grelot. *What Are the Targums? Selected Texts.* Old Testament Studies 7. Translated by S. Attanasio. Collegeville, Minn.: Liturgical, 1992. Original title: *Les Targoums.* Paris: Cerf, 1992.

From the biblical Targums, the compiler has chosen sixty passages—many of which are little known or scattered in rare and scholarly works—to translate into English.

**109** W. Richter. *Biblia Hebraica Transcripta.* 16 vols. Arbeiten zu Text und Sprache im Alten Testament 33. St. Ottilien, Germany: EOS, 1991–93.

These Old Testament fascicles (including one for Sirach or Ecclesiasticus) place the Hebrew script and a sophisticated transliteration onto facing pages. Every phrase or clause appears on a separate line.

**110** M. McNamara (ed.). *The Aramaic Bible: The Targums.* 19 vols. Wilmington, Del.: Glazier, 1987– .

Based on the best critical editions available, this series will freshly translate all extant Targums of the Old Testament into English.

**111** I. Drazin, M. Aberbach, and B. Grossfeld. *Targum Onkelos.* 5 vols. Hoboken: Ktav, 1982– .

The editors comment on this Pentateuchal Targum and render it into English. The Aramaic and English texts face one another on opposite pages.

**112** J. R. Kohlenberger III (ed.). *The NIV Triglot Old Testament.* Grand Rapids: Zondervan, 1981.

This tome lays the Masoretic Text (Hebrew), Septuagint (Greek), and New International Version (English) in three parallel columns.

**113** M. L. Klein. *The Fragment-Targums of the Pentateuch.* 2 vols. Analecta Biblica 76. Rome: Biblical Institute, 1980.

In volume two, the author has prepared a full English translation for each of the four major texts of the so-called Fragmentary Targum of the Pentateuch.

**114** J. R. Kohlenberger III. *The NIV Interlinear Hebrew-English Old Testament.* 4 vols. Grand Rapids: Zondervan, 1979–85.

This book basically supplies a shortcut for students. It records the text of the Hebrew Bible and gives a literal English translation directly beneath each word.

**115** E. C. Ulrich, Jr. *The Qumran Text of Samuel and Josephus.* Harvard Semitic Monographs 19. Missoula, Mont.: Scholars, 1978.

This work includes parts of 1–2 Samuel as found among the Hebrew manuscripts from Qumran Cave 4.

**116** M. H. Goshen-Gottstein (ed.). *The Aleppo Codex.* Jerusalem: Magnes, 1976.

This is a facsimile of the Hebrew codex considered authoritative by Maimonides. It was pointed allegedly by Aaron ben Asher and provided with Masoretic notes.

**117** J. P. Green, Sr. *The Interlinear Bible.* 4 vols. Wilmington, Del.: Associated, 1976–79. Reprinted Grand Rapids: Baker, 1986.

The first three volumes, on the Old Testament, contain an acceptable Hebrew-to-English translation printed both in interlinear fashion and alongside the main text in paragraph form.

**118** M. H. Goshen-Gottstein (ed.). *Hebrew University Bible.* Jerusalem: Magnes, 1975– .

This very detailed publication of the Hebrew Bible will include the large and small Masora as well as a critical apparatus reflecting the history of the text.

**119** *The Book of Ben Sira: Text, Concordance and an Analysis of the Vocabulary* (in Hebrew). Historical Dictionary of the Hebrew Language. Jerusalem: Academy of the Hebrew Language, 1973.

This is an excellent modern Hebrew study containing the ancient Hebrew text of Sirach (Ecclesiasticus).

**120** B. Grossfeld (ed.). *The Targum to the Five Megilloth.* New York: Hermon, 1973.

The editor has rendered the Targum of Ruth, Canticles, Ecclesiastes, Lamentations, and Esther into English.

**121** *Pentateuch, Prophets and Hagiographa: Codex Leningrad B 19$^A$.* 3 vols. Jerusalem: Makor, 1971.

This is a facsimile edition of the earliest complete Hebrew Bible manuscript, at the end of which incidentally are lists preserving information on the Ben-Asher system of vocalization and its stages of development.

**122** J. Macdonald. *The Samaritan Chronicle No. II.* Beihefte zur Zeitschrift für die alttestamentliche Wissenschaft 107. Berlin: de Gruyter, 1969.

This scholar has edited a Samaritan Hebrew text that comprises much of the following books: Joshua, Judges, 1–2 Samuel, 1–2 Kings, and 1–2 Chronicles.

**123** A. Díez Macho (ed.). *Neophyti 1: Targum Palestinense.* 6 vols. Textos y estudios del Seminario Filológico Cardenal Cisneros 7–11 and 20. Madrid: CSIC, 1968–79.

An ancient Targum of the Pentateuch appears, accompanied by modern translations of the Targum into English as well as French and Spanish.

**124**  F. Vattioni (ed.). *Ecclesiastico.* Pubblicazioni del Seminario di Semitistica, Testi 1. Naples: Istituto Orientale, 1968.

This handy edition of Sirach (Ecclesiasticus) contains the Hebrew text with a critical apparatus and the ancient Greek, Syriac, and Latin versions.

**125**  K. Elliger and W. Rudolph (eds.). *Biblia Hebraica Stuttgartensia.* Stuttgart: Deutsche Bibelstiftung, 1967–77.

Currently this is the standard critical edition of the Hebrew and Aramaic Old Testament. Masoretic notes and a critical apparatus supplement the printed biblical text.

**126**  Y. Yadin. *The Ben Sira Scroll from Masada.* Jerusalem: Israel Exploration Society, 1965.

The editor has published fragments from Masada that bear the Hebrew text of Sirach (Ecclesiasticus) 39:27–43:30.

**127**  C. A. Muses (ed.). *The Septuagint Bible: The Oldest Text of the Old Testament.* 2d ed. Indian Hills, Colo.: Falcon's, 1960.

The editor excludes the apocrypha/deuterocanonicals. Otherwise, this tome is of value both to general readers without knowledge of Greek and to scholars for quick and easy reference.

**128**  F. Pérez Castro. *Séfer Abiša<sup>c</sup>: Edición del fragmento antiguo del rollo sagrado del Pentateuco hebreo Samaritano de Nablus.* Textos y estudios del Seminario Filológico Cardenal Cisneros 2. Madrid: CSIC, 1959.

This scholar has published an edition of the most famous copy of the Samaritan Pentateuch. The Hebrew text runs from Numbers 35 to Deuteronomy 34.

**129**  N. H. Snaith (ed.). *Hebrew Old Testament.* London: British and Foreign Bible Society, 1958.

The Hebrew text in this handy edition—which omits any critical apparatus—differs little from that in either *Biblia Hebraica* (#132) or *Biblia Hebraica Stuttgartensia* (#125).

**130**  G. M. Lamsa. *The Holy Bible from Ancient Eastern Manuscripts.* Philadelphia: Holman, 1957. Reprinted San Francisco: Harper, 1985.

The editor offers a usually reliable translation of the Syriac Peshitta into English.

**131** R. A. Knox. *The Old Testament*. 2 vols. New York: Sheed, 1948–50. London: Burns, 1949.

This is the Old Testament portion of the Latin Vulgate translated into English.

**132** R. Kittel (ed.). *Biblia Hebraica*. 3d ed. Stuttgart: Württembergische Bibelanstalt, 1937.

Major revision in the third edition was followed in subsequent printings of this now-superseded Hebrew Bible (see #125) by errors being corrected and variants from relevant Dead Sea Scrolls being inserted.

**133** A. Rahlfs (ed.). *Septuaginta*. 2 vols. Stuttgart: Württembergische Bibelanstalt, 1935.

The most convenient and popular of all editions of the Septuagint, this work is intended to serve the needs of pastors and students.

**134** J. Marcus. *The Newly Discovered Original Hebrew of Ben Sira*. Philadelphia: Dropsie, 1931.

Along with notes and an English translation, the editor published the Hebrew text of Ecclesiasticus or Sirach 32:16–34:1, a manuscript section previously missing.

**135** *Septuaginta: Vetus Testamentum Graecum*. 16 vols. Göttingen: Vandenhoeck, 1931– .

This ongoing series aims to reconstruct an Old Testament text whose readings at each point seem best in light of the Greek manuscript evidence as a whole. A detailed critical apparatus emphasizes families or groups of manuscripts.

**136** A. von Gall (ed.). *Der hebräische Pentateuch der Samaritaner*. 5 vols. Giessen: Töpelmann, 1914–18. Reprinted Berlin: de Gruyter, 1966.

This is an eclectic edition of the Hebrew text of the Pentateuch according to the Samaritan tradition.

**137** C. D. Ginsburg (ed.). *The Old Testament*. 4 vols. London: British and Foreign Bible Society, 1908–26. Reprinted Jerusalem: Makor, 1969–70.

The editor of this Hebrew Bible has incorporated a massive amount of Masoretic material and minute manuscript variations.

**138** H. B. Swete (ed.). *The Old Testament in Greek*. 3d–4th ed. 3 vols. Cambridge: Cambridge University, 1907–12.

One may have to consult this work for textual-critical projects involving biblical books not yet published in the Cambridge (#139) or Göttingen (#135) sets.

**139** A. E. Brooke, N. McLean, and H. S. J. Thackeray (eds.). *The Old Testament in Greek*. 3 vols. Cambridge: Cambridge University, 1906–40.

The large pages of this indispensable tool hold an extensive critical apparatus. Sadly, the set is incomplete and covers only from Genesis to Tobit in the Septuagint sequence.

**140** I. Lévi (ed.). *The Hebrew Text of the Book of Ecclesiasticus*. Semitic Study Series 3. Leiden: Brill, 1904.

This edition of the extant Hebrew portions of Sirach, or Ecclesiasticus, includes brief notes on the textual readings.

**141** S. Schechter and C. Taylor (eds.). *The Wisdom of Ben Sira*. New York: Macmillan/Cambridge: Cambridge University, 1899. Reprinted Amsterdam: APA, 1979.

This is the first printed edition of the major Hebrew fragments of Sirach (Ecclesiasticus) discovered in the Cairo Geniza.

**142** J. W. Etheridge. *The Targums of Onkelos and Jonathan ben Uzziel on the Pentateuch*. 2 vols. London: Longman, 1862–65. Reprinted New York: Ktav, 1968.

The editor has translated the Onqelos and Pseudo-Jonathan Targums of the Pentateuch into English.

**143** L. C. L. Brenton. *The Septuagint Version of the Old Testament*. London: Bagster, 1844. Reprinted *The Septuagint with Apocrypha: Greek and English*. Peabody: Hendrickson, 1987.

This tome features the Septuagint in parallel columns with an English translation of it.

**144**  R. Holmes and J. Parsons (eds.). *Vetus Testamentum Graecum cum variis lectionibus.* 5 vols. Oxford: Clarendon, 1798–1827.

> The editors provided the first really comprehensive, critical treatment of the entire Septuagint. Although quite out-of-date, the work is a storehouse of information.

## 2.2 Studies

Explanations of the art and science of textual criticism, analyses of the translation technique of the Septuagint, aids to employing critical editions of the Old Testament/Hebrew Bible, studies about the Samaritan Pentateuch, and the like, make up the contents of this section.

**145**  E. R. Brotzman. *Old Testament Textual Criticism: A Practical Introduction.* Grand Rapids: Baker, 1994.

> The author nicely accomplishes his primary goal of leading students through the steps involved in using the textual-critical data recorded in the Stuttgart Hebrew Bible (#125) so as to evaluate variant readings.

**146**  A. Aejmelaeus. *On the Trail of the Septuagint Translators: Collected Essays.* Kampen, Netherlands: Pharos, 1993.

> Each essay studies the techniques of the Septuagint translators, discusses phenomena found in their Koine Greek, and explains the ways they handled Hebrew idioms.

**147**  G. J. Brooke and B. Lindars (eds.). *Septuagint, Scrolls, and Cognate Writings.* Society of Biblical Literature Septuagint and Cognate Studies 33. Atlanta: Scholars, 1992.

> This book contains papers presented by seventeen commentators in 1990 at Manchester, England, to an international symposium on the Septuagint and its relationship to the Dead Sea Scrolls and other writings.

**148**  E. Tov. *Textual Criticism of the Hebrew Bible.* Minneapolis: Fortress/Maastricht: Van Gorcum, 1992.

> The author offers extensive descriptions of the major witnesses to the Old Testament text and pays special attention to the problem of its original shape.

**149**  S. Olofsson. *The LXX Version: A Guide to the Translation Technique of the Septuagint.* Coniectanea Biblica Old Testament Series 30. Stockholm: Almqvist, 1990.

The writer outlines a methodological approach for comparing the Septuagint with the Masoretic Text and evaluates resources for studying the translation in the Greek Old Testament.

**150**  R. Wonneberger. *Understanding BHS: A Manual for the Users of "Biblia Hebraica Stuttgartensia."* Translated by D. R. Daniels. 2d ed. Subsidia Biblica 8. Rome: Biblical Institute, 1990. Original title: *Leitfaden zur "Biblia Hebraica Stuttgartensia."* Göttingen: Vandenhoeck, 1986.

By plainly elucidating the characteristics of the critical apparatus, the author enables beginners as well as experts to use its complex data for textual and exegetical work.

**151**  F. E. Deist. *Witnesses to the Old Testament: Introducing Old Testament Textual Criticism.* The Literature of the Old Testament 5. Pretoria: Kerkboekhandel, 1988.

This stimulating work discusses the history and aims of the field, surveys Hebrew textual witnesses and ancient translations, and even deals with modern editions of the Hebrew Bible.

**152**  W. R. Scott. *A Simplified Guide to BHS.* Berkeley: BIBAL, 1987.

The author has gathered into one place simple instructions for understanding the critical apparatus, Masoretic notes, and other markings in the Stuttgart Old Testament (#125).

**153**  R. Kraft and E. Tov (eds.). *Computer Assisted Tools for Septuagint Studies.* Atlanta: Scholars, 1986– .

This project came into existence as a means toward producing a lexicon for the Septuagint. However, the results also aid textual criticism: namely, reconstructing and comparing Hebrew and Greek texts.

**154**  P. K. McCarter, Jr. *Textual Criticism: Recovering the Text of the Hebrew Bible.* Guides to Biblical Scholarship. Philadelphia: Fortress, 1986.

The author elaborates on the work involved in the critical evaluation of a given portion of text and illustrates his explanations with carefully selected examples of the phenomena treated.

**155** J. J. McGann. *A Critique of Modern Textual Criticism*. Chicago: University of Chicago, 1983. Reprinted Charlottesville: University of Virginia, 1992.

In this compelling book the writer sets biblical (as well as classical) textual criticism within a broader perspective and discusses certain recent theoretical questions.

**156** R. I. Vasholz. *Data for the Sigla of the BHS*. Winona Lake, Ind.: Eisenbrauns, 1983.

In a tabular arrangement, this eight-page compendium displays dates, languages, and explanations for the manuscripts cited in the Stuttgart Bible's (#125) critical apparatus.

**157** J. Weingreen. *Introduction to the Critical Study of the Text of the Hebrew Bible*. Oxford: Clarendon, 1982.

The author's practical explanations will enable students at a minimum to follow a standard critical commentary on the Hebrew text. One intriguing chapter outlines rabbinic antecedents of textual criticism.

**158** C. McCarthy. *The Tiqqune Sopherim and Other Theological Corrections in the Masoretic Text of the Old Testament*. Orbis Biblicus et Orientalis 36. Fribourg: Universitätsverlag/Göttingen: Vandenhoeck, 1981.

The aim of this study is to examine whether, and to what extent, the custodians of the sacred text did actively emend certain passages for theological motives.

**159** H. P. Rüger. *An English Key to the Latin Words and Abbreviations and the Symbols of "Biblia Hebraica Stuttgartensia."* Stuttgart: German Bible Society, 1981.

This small brochure presents the Latin expressions of the critical apparatus in alphabetical order and supplies each with an English translation and a passage where used.

**160** E. Tov. *The Text-Critical Use of the Septuagint in Biblical Research*. Jerusalem Biblical Studies 3. Jerusalem: Simor, 1981.

This methodological handbook is an important modern work on the Septuagint and its role in the study of the Hebrew Scriptures.

**161** I. Yeivin. *Introduction to the Tiberian Masorah*. Translated by E. J. Revell. Masoretic Studies 5. Missoula, Mont.: Scholars, 1980. Original title: *Idem* (in Hebrew). Jerusalem: Hebrew University, 1971.

This excellent, up-to-date study demonstrates the early origin and complex development of the Masoretic tradition and describes its resultant notes and signs.

**162** E. Würthwein. *The Text of the Old Testament: An Introduction to the Biblia Hebraica*. Translated by E. F. Rhodes. Grand Rapids: Eerdmans, 1979. London: SCM, 1980. Original title: *Der Text des Alten Testaments*. Stuttgart: Deutsche Bibelgesellschaft, 1988.

This book describes the various Old Testament texts and versions and tells about their origins and histories. Very helpful explanations accompany reproductions from several dozen important manuscripts.

**163** F. E. Deist. *Towards the Text of the Old Testament*. Translated by W. K. Winckler. Pretoria: Church, 1978.

This systematic introduction to the field of textual criticism has served as a university textbook. In presenting controversial matters, the author allows many points of view to speak.

**164** E. J. Revell. *Biblical Texts with Palestinian Pointing and Their Accents*. Masoretic Studies 4. Missoula, Mont.: Scholars, 1977.

The writer devotes the greater part of his book to accentuation, but the closing section concerns the relationship of the Palestinian pointing as a whole to the Tiberian.

**165** F. M. Cross and S. Talmon (eds.). *Qumran and the History of the Biblical Text*. Cambridge: Harvard University, 1975.

This very serviceable collection of writings (most previously published) considers how the discovery of Old Testament manuscripts at Qumran has affected the status of the Masoretic Text and the Septuagint.

**166** S. Jellicoe (comp.). *Studies in the Septuagint: Origins, Recensions, and Interpretations.* Library of Biblical Studies. New York: Ktav, 1974.

The compiler has assembled almost three dozen valuable articles about the Greek Old Testament: its translation, transmission, usage, significance, and so forth.

**167** R. W. Klein. *Textual Criticism of the Old Testament: The Septuagint after Qumran.* Guides to Biblical Scholarship. Philadelphia: Fortress, 1974.

In a manner easy to read and not overly technical, the writer explains the complex relations between the Masoretic Text, the Hebrew manuscripts presupposed by the Septuagint, and the biblical documents from the Qumran caves.

**168** S. Z. Leiman (ed.). *The Canon and Masorah of the Hebrew Bible: An Introductory Reader.* Library of Biblical Studies. New York: Ktav, 1974.

While this collection of noteworthy papers investigates (as suggested by the title) both the canon and the text of the Old Testament, the bulk of the book concentrates on textual-critical issues.

**169** *Preliminary and Interim Report on the Hebrew Old Testament Text Project.* 5 vols. New York: United Bible Societies, 1973–80.

This set makes available to Bible translators and scholars a wide range of exegetically relevant textual problems along with suggested solutions and reasons for the textual decisions.

**170** P. Walters. *The Text of the Septuagint: Its Corruptions and Their Emendation.* Edited by D. W. Gooding. London: Cambridge University, 1973.

Unfortunately, this work progressed far enough to cover only "corruptions" (not "emendation"): both grammatical corruptions—such as in vowels, consonants, and word formation—and Hebraisms—transliterations, borrowings, and so forth.

**171**   G. E. Weil. *Massorah Gedolah iuxta Codicem Leningraden-sem B 19a.* 4 vols. Rome: Biblical Institute, 1971– .

This is an elaborate project on the Masoretic notes in the medieval text of the Hebrew Bible. So far only volume one has appeared, which catalogs the large Masora's lists.

**172**   P. Williams, Jr. *An English Key to the Symbols and Latin Words and Abbreviations of "Biblia Hebraica."* Stuttgart: Württembergische Bibelanstalt, 1969.

This convenient English pamphlet interprets both the Latin abbreviations conveying information about variant readings and the signs representing major manuscripts and versions.

**173**   S. Jellicoe. *The Septuagint and Modern Study.* Oxford: Clarendon, 1968. Reprinted Ann Arbor: Eisenbrauns, 1978.

This introduction addresses the origins of the Septuagint and its transmission history as well as its text and language. The volume includes a very thorough bibliography.

**174**   J. D. Purvis. *The Samaritan Pentateuch and the Origin of the Samaritan Sect.* Harvard Semitic Monographs 2. Cambridge: Harvard University, 1968.

This modern study describes the evidence newly brought to light about the formation of the Samaritan pentateuchal tradition and its link with the emergence of the Samaritan faction.

**175**   D. R. Ap-Thomas. *A Primer of Old Testament Text Criticism.* 2d ed. Oxford: Blackwell, 1965. Philadelphia: Fortress, 1966.

For students and laypeople this introduction treats the standardization of the text, the ancient versions, the work of the Masoretes, and the types of manuscript errors.

**176**   P. E. Kahle. *The Cairo Geniza.* 2d ed. New York: Praeger/ Oxford: Blackwell, 1959.

With special interest in differing systems of punctuation, the author discusses the text of the Hebrew Bible and its ancient translations—particularly in light of manuscripts from Cairo and Qumran.

**177** B. J. Roberts. *The Old Testament Text and Versions: The Hebrew Text in Transmission and the History of the Ancient Versions.* Cardiff: University of Wales, 1951.

Though now old, this careful analysis contains much basic information and terminology about the Hebrew text and its problems and about the ancient translations.

**178** L. Goldschmidt. *The Earliest Editions of the Hebrew Bible.* New York: Aldus, 1950.

Besides an informative treatise on the oldest manuscripts of the Masoretic Text, this volume affords extensive data on fifteenth- and sixteenth-century printings of the Hebrew Bible or portions thereof.

**179** H. M. Orlinsky. *The Septuagint: The Oldest Translation of the Bible.* Union Anniversary Series. Cincinnati: Union of American Hebrew Congregations, 1949.

Among numerous other things, the author answers why later Jews rejected the Septuagint and by what external features the Greek Old Testament differs from the Hebrew Bible.

**180** R. Gordis. *The Biblical Text in the Making: A Study of the Kethib-Qere.* Philadelphia: Dropsie College, 1937. Reprinted New York: Ktav, 1971.

Hoping to contribute to a better understanding of the role of the Masora, the writer investigates the Kethib-Qere phenomenon—that is, the origin and nature of these variant readings.

**181** R. R. Ottley. *A Handbook to the Septuagint.* London: Methuen, 1920.

This comprehensive introduction to the Septuagint demands some prior knowledge of the Greek language and the Old Testament. A reference glossary identifies names and terms.

**182** H. B. Swete. *An Introduction to the Old Testament in Greek.* Revised by R. R. Ottley. 2d ed. New York: Putnam/ Cambridge: Cambridge University, 1914. Reprinted Peabody: Hendrickson, 1990.

This classic volume concerns itself with the history, contents, textual condition, and literary use of the Septuagint. The "Letter of Aristeas" appears in an appendix.

**183** C. D. Ginsburg. *Introduction to the Massoretico-Critical Edition of the Hebrew Bible*. London: Trinitarian Bible Society, 1897. Reprinted New York: Ktav, 1966.

Although prepared specifically for the author's own edition of the Old Testament (#137), this tome is a fountainhead of information on the Masoretic Text for scholars, whatever edition they utilize.

# 3

# Language

## 3.1 Lexicons

The items enumerated below entail full-scale dictionaries, analyzed vocabularies, and simple word lists that are based on the Hebrew and Aramaic of the Masoretic Text and the Samaritan Pentateuch as well as the Greek of the Septuagint. The section also incorporates several topical investigations: for example, hapax legomena.

**184** D. J. A. Clines (ed.). *The Dictionary of Classical Hebrew.* 8 vols. Sheffield: JSOT, 1993– .

This dictionary will be the first ever compiled for classical Hebrew as a whole: that is, the language found in the Bible (including Sirach, or Ecclesiasticus), the Dead Sea Scrolls, and other writings down to around A.D. 200.

**185** L. Koehler, W. Baumgartner, and J. J. Stamm. *The Hebrew and Aramaic Lexicon of the Old Testament.* Translated by M. E. J. Richardson. 3 vols. Leiden: Brill, 1993– . Original title: *Hebräisches und aramäisches Lexikon zum Alten Testament.* Leiden: Brill, 1967– .

This standard reference tool contains the complete vocabulary of the Masoretic Text, extended with variants from the Oriental and Samaritan textual traditions, the fragments of Sirach (Ecclesiasticus), the Dead Sea Scrolls, and so forth. The editors have arranged the entries in a strictly alphabetical sequence rather than by verbal roots.

**186**  T. Muraoka. *A Greek-English Lexicon of the Septuagint (Twelve Prophets)*. Leuven: Peeters, 1993.

This is the first installment of a full-fledged Septuagintal lexicon. It presents a wealth of orthographic, morphologic, syntactic, semantic, and idiomatic information for every word—including such high-frequency words as prepositions and conjunctions.

**187**  B. A. Taylor. *The Analytical Lexicon to the Septuagint: A Complete Parsing Guide*. Grand Rapids: Zondervan, 1993.

This tool, which is designed to assist students in reading the Septuagint with greater speed and accuracy, describes in alphabetical sequence the form of every word found there.

**188**  L. Glinert. *The Joys of Hebrew*. New York: Oxford University, 1992.

The author supplies brief definitions for over six hundred Hebrew terms and expressions and then illustrates their usage with generous excerpts from the Bible and Talmud as well as from modern written works.

**189**  J. Lust, E. Eynikel, and K. Hauspie (eds.). *A Greek-English Lexicon of the Septuagint*. 2 vols. Stuttgart: Deutsche Bibelgesellschaft, 1992– .

A thorough research tool for one's study of the Septuagint, this lexicon with insightful entries includes a helpful introduction and bibliography.

**190**  F. I. Andersen and A. D. Forbes. *The Vocabulary of the Old Testament*. Rome: Biblical Institute, 1989.

This reference work is designed for easy and accurate access to information on the distribution of the Old Testament's Hebrew and Aramaic vocabulary. The authors provide concise English glosses and part-of-speech assignments, too.

**191**  J. J. Owens. *Analytical Key to the Old Testament*. 4 vols. Grand Rapids: Baker, 1989–92.

Moving through the Old Testament verse by verse, this tool gives every word or phrase its grammatical identification and an English translation.

**192** F. Rehkopf. *Septuaginta-Vokabular.* Göttingen: Vandenhoeck, 1989.

This statistical analysis exhibits the entire vocabulary of the Septuagint in a columnar arrangement. The layout permits ready identification of the Hebrew or Aramaic equivalents and calls attention to employment in the New Testament, too.

**193** J. P. Green, Sr. (ed.). *A Concise Lexicon to the Biblical Languages.* Peabody: Hendrickson, 1987.

For the words of both the Old and New Testaments, this book gives meanings, parts of speech, gender, and scriptural examples, besides page numbers in other reference works where more information can be obtained.

**194** E. D. Klein. *A Comprehensive Etymological Dictionary of the Hebrew Language.* New York: Macmillan/London: Collier/Jerusalem: Carta, 1987.

Although focusing on modern Hebrew, the writer details how scriptural terms have informed today's language.

**195** R. Meyer and H. Donner (eds.). *Hebräisches und aramäisches Handwörterbuch über das Alte Testament.* 18th ed. Berlin: Springer, 1987– .

Written in German only, this volume emerges approximately seven decades after the previous edition in the line of lexicons started by Wilhelm Gesenius. The present revision takes into account both our improved understanding of Semitic languages (including Hebrew) and our discovery of new ones (for example, Ugaritic).

**196** T. S. Beall, W. A. Banks, and C. Smith. *Old Testament Parsing Guide.* 2 vols. Chicago: Moody, 1986–90.

This guide, which parses every Old Testament verb by occurrence, helps whenever an interpreter cannot otherwise identify a verbal root.

**197** F. E. Greenspahn. *Hapax Legomena in Biblical Hebrew: A Study of the Phenomenon and Its Treatment since Antiq-*

*uity.* SBL Dissertation Series 74. Chico, Calif.: Scholars, 1984.

> The author surveys interpretations made by ancient versions, rabbinic commentators, and medieval and modern exegetes of verbal forms among "absolute" hapax legomena in the Old Testament.

**198** L. A. Mitchel. *A Student's Vocabulary for Biblical Hebrew and Aramaic.* Grand Rapids: Zondervan, 1984.

> The writer lists every biblical Hebrew word appearing ten or more times and all biblical Aramaic words. Besides basic definitions and frequency counts, guides to phonetic pronunciation accompany the words.

**199** M. A. Robinson (comp.). *Indexes to All Editions of Brown-Driver-Briggs Hebrew Lexicon and Thayer's Greek Lexicon.* Grand Rapids: Baker, 1981.

> In its first section, this index assists even students who do not know Hebrew in finding the location (page and column) of a particular word's handling in the lexicon by Brown and others (#219).

**200** T. A. Armstrong, D. L. Busby, and C. F. Carr. *A Reader's Hebrew-English Lexicon of the Old Testament.* 4 vols. Grand Rapids: Zondervan, 1980–88.

> These volumes give definitions for any Hebrew words occurring less than fifty times in the Old Testament, in order as the words appear verse by verse. The purpose is to increase a beginner's speed in reading.

**201** W. Bauer, W. F. Arndt, F. W. Gingrich, and F. W. Danker. *A Greek-English Lexicon of the New Testament and Other Early Christian Literature.* 2d ed. Chicago: University of Chicago, 1979.

> While this is a dictionary of the Church's early writings, we may consult it for the Old Testament because many New Testament words had previously been used in the Septuagint with similar significations.

**202** H. R. Cohen. *Biblical Hapax Legomena in the Light of Akkadian and Ugaritic.* SBL Dissertation Series 37. Missoula, Mont.: Scholars, 1978.

The author lists all hapax legomena of the Old Testament and discusses those that have reasonably certain cognates in Akkadian or Ugaritic.

**203** B. Einspahr. *Index to Brown, Driver & Briggs Hebrew Lexicon.* Rev. ed. Chicago: Moody, 1977.

Proceeding from Genesis to Malachi, this work records the precise page and section location in the dictionary by Brown and others (#219) whenever an entry in that lexicon cites a specific scriptural passage's use of a Hebrew or Aramaic term.

**204** R. Renehan. *Greek Lexicographical Notes: A Critical Supplement to the Greek-English Lexicon of Liddell-Scott-Jones.* 2 vols. Hypomnemata 45 and 74. Göttingen: Vandenhoeck, 1975–82.

This work consists of material on a collection of vocabulary entries that were either documented inadequately or omitted in the lexicon by Liddell and others (#217; cf. #210).

**205** G. Fohrer (ed.). *Hebrew and Aramaic Dictionary of the Old Testament.* Translated by W. Johnstone. London: SCM, 1973. Original title: *Hebräisches und aramäisches Wörterbuch zum Alten Testament.* Berlin: de Gruyter, 1989.

For the purpose of simple translation—as opposed to serious exegesis—of Old Testament texts, this handy dictionary provides definitions (and occasionally indications of scriptural passages) for all biblical Hebrew and Aramaic terms, including names.

**206** X. Jacques. *List of Septuagint Words Sharing Common Elements.* Subsidia Biblica 1. Rome: Biblical Institute, 1972.

This enumeration of words that share common elements with other words in the Septuagint allows for interesting observations to be made in the field of biblical lexicography.

**207** C. A. Wahl and J. B. Bauer. *Clavis Librorum Veteris Testamenti Apocryphorum Philologica.* Graz: Akademische, 1972.

This book illustrates the vocabulary of the apocrypha and pseudepigrapha in the Septuagint by comparison with examples drawn from classical Greek writers.

**208** W. L. Holladay. *A Concise Hebrew and Aramaic Lexicon of the Old Testament.* Grand Rapids: Eerdmans/Leiden: Brill, 1971.

The editor abridged the Old Testament dictionary by Koehler and others (#185). The resultant volume is well suited for students starting their study of biblical Hebrew or Aramaic.

**209** E. Vogt (ed.). *Lexicon Linguae Aramaicae Veteris Testamenti.* Rome: Biblical Institute, 1971.

The author of this outstanding dictionary, penned in Latin, abundantly illustrates the words in biblical Aramaic with usages of the same terms in nonbiblical Aramaic texts.

**210** E. A. Barber, P. Maas, M. Scheller, and M. L. West (eds.). *Greek-English Lexicon: A Supplement.* Oxford: Clarendon, 1968.

This product seeks primarily to note linguistic knowledge gleaned from Greek inscriptions and papyri that were discovered since completion of the dictionary by Liddell and others (#217).

**211** G. M. Landes. *A Student's Vocabulary of Biblical Hebrew.* New York: Scribner's, 1961.

The editor advantageously groups the words by verbal cognate (when extant in the Old Testament) as well as by frequency of occurrence. An index facilitates the rapid location of individual Hebrew terms.

**212** A. Murtonen. *An Etymological Vocabulary to the Samaritan Pentateuch.* Studia Orientalia 24. Vol. 2 of *Materials for a Non-Masoretic Hebrew Grammar.* Helsinki: Finnish Oriental Society, 1960.

This lexicon, which writes the words in transliteration and groups them by root, states their meanings generally only where different from those of the corresponding words in the Masoretic Text.

**213** J. D. W. Watts. *Lists of Words Occurring Frequently in the Hebrew Bible.* 2d ed. Grand Rapids: Eerdmans, 1960. Leiden: Brill, 1967.

> Separating verbs, nouns, and particles into three distinct series, the author presents biblical Hebrew vocabulary quite compactly and provides stem/pattern indications for the verbs where appropriate.

**214** K. G. Kuhn. *Retrograde Hebrew Lexicon.* Göttingen: Vandenhoeck, 1958.

> The editor has taken the Hebrew words of the Masoretic Text, Sirach (Ecclesiasticus), and extrabiblical manuscripts from Qumran Cave 1 and alphabetized them in backward spelling. The purpose is to aid the filling in of Dead Sea Scroll lacunas where only the final letters of a term appear.

**215** J. B. Payne. *Hebrew Vocabularies.* Grand Rapids: Baker, 1956.

> The editor orders biblical Hebrew words alphabetically within categories of descending frequency and presents particles in a particularly helpful way.

**216** F. Zorell (ed.). *Lexicon Hebraicum Veteris Testamenti.* Rome: Biblical Institute, 1940–84.

> This noteworthy Old Testament lexicon—written in Latin—possesses many good observations, plus a commendable handling of the Hebrew diction in Sirach, or Ecclesiasticus.

**217** H. G. Liddell, R. Scott, H. S. Jones, and R. McKenzie. *A Greek-English Lexicon.* 9th ed. 2 vols. Oxford: Clarendon, 1925–40.

> Though mainly devoted to the classical language, this excellent lexicon frequently adduces examples of word utilization in the Septuagint and always discusses the history of any Greek word.

**218** E. Ben-Yehuda. *A Complete Dictionary of Ancient and Modern Hebrew* (in Hebrew). 16 vols. Berlin: Langenscheidt, 1908–59. Reprinted New York: Yoseloff, 1960.

> Because it shows the history of a word, this lexicon of the Hebrew language often contributes toward problem solv-

ing in the interpretation of biblical passages. Additionally, the author gives the basic meaning of each word in English, French, and German.

**219** F. Brown, S. R. Driver, and C. A. Briggs. *A Hebrew and English Lexicon of the Old Testament.* Boston: Houghton, 1906. Oxford: Clarendon, 1907. Reprinted *The New Brown-Driver-Briggs-Gesenius Hebrew and English Lexicon.* Peabody: Hendrickson, 1979.

A classic Old Testament lexicon written in English, it unfortunately does not (and could not) reflect the lexicographical advances made this century. Yet, among other things, the book's treatment of both biblical Hebrew and Aramaic idioms renders it still valuable.

**220** B. Davidson. *The Analytical Hebrew and Chaldee Lexicon.* 2d ed. London: Bagster, 1855. Reprinted Peabody: Hendrickson, 1986.

Every biblical Hebrew and Aramaic word or inflection is alphabetically listed exactly as it appears in the Masoretic Text, along with a grammatical analysis and an indication of the root.

**221** J. F. Schleusner. *Novus Thesaurus Philologico-criticus.* 2d ed. 3 vols. London: Duncan, 1829.

The value of this resource, penned in Latin, derives principally from its being the only complete lexicon to the Septuagint in existence.

## 3.2 Concordances

There are concordances for the Masoretic Text; there are those for the Septuagint—including the apocryphal/deuterocanonical books. Another concordance deals with the Hebrew manuscripts of Sirach, or Ecclesiasticus. Still another lists entries by subject.

**222** E. Katz (ed.). *A New Classified Concordance of the Bible.* Jerusalem: Kiryat-Sefer, 1992.

Usable to readers of either Hebrew or English, this concordance organizes nearly 36,000 Old Testament passages under an array of topical and subtopical headings covering such areas as plants, religion, and measurements.

**223** A. Even-Shoshan (ed.). *A New Concordance of the Bible.* New ed. Jerusalem: Kiryat-Sefer, 1989.

Word-frequency counts, fully vocalized context citations, and the inclusion of common phrases in addition to individual Hebrew and Aramaic terms are among the innovative features of this tome on the Old Testament.

**224** T. Muraoka. *A Greek-Hebrew/Aramaic Index to I Esdras.* Septuagint and Cognate Studies 16. Chico, Calif.: Scholars, 1984.

The author lists the Greek words found in the apocryphal/deuterocanonical book of 1 Esdras. For each occurrence, the index shows the corresponding Hebrew or Aramaic term from the passage's counterpart in the (proto)canonical books of Ezra, Nehemiah, and Chronicles.

**225** Benedictine Monks of Maredsous in Belgium. *Concordantia Polyglotta: La concordance de la Bible.* 5 vols. Oxford: Blackwell, 1981– .

This is a computer-generated comparative tabulation of words and expressions from the books of the Bible in various editions and versions, including the Masoretic Text and Septuagint.

**226** L. T. Whitelocke (ed.). *An Analytical Concordance of the Books of the Apocrypha.* Washington: University Press of America, 1978.

The editor has produced a complete concordance to the apocryphal/deuterocanonical books of the Old Testament. Although the volume is keyed to English words, it does list the Greek equivalents.

**227** D. Barthélemy and O. Rickenbacher (eds.). *Konkordanz zum hebräischen Sirach.* Göttingen: Vandenhoeck, 1973.

For every Hebrew entry, the editors display the context(s) in which it appears, describe the grammatical form(s) of the word, and state the matching term(s) used in the Greek and Syriac versions.

**228** J. A. Baird and D. N. Freedman (eds.). *The Computer Bible*. Missoula, Mont.: Scholars, 1971– .

The volumes in this long-range concordance project on both the Old and New Testaments consist of relevant morphological, syntactic, and semantic data placed opposite each word and reference in parallel columns.

**229** J. Reider. *Index to Aquila*. Revised by N. Turner. Supplements to Vetus Testamentum 12. Leiden: Brill, 1966.

This index to Aquila's Greek version of the Old Testament functions to assist in the task of obtaining a pre-Masoretic Hebrew text. Proper names, certain particles and prepositions, and the definite article are enumerated along with common words.

**230** S. Mandelkern. *Veteris Testamenti Concordantiae Hebraicae atque Chaldaicae*. Edited by M. H. Goshen-Gottstein. 3d ed. Tel Aviv: Schocken, 1959.

This excellent and detailed volume groups citations from the Old Testament according to sense. Within that arrangement occurrences of the Hebrew or Aramaic word itself are listed first, then occurrences of the term with its prefixal and suffixal augments.

**231** G. Lisowsky and L. Rost. *Konkordanz zum hebräischen Alten Testament*. Stuttgart: Württembergische Bibelanstalt, 1958.

This convenient reference book of legibly handwritten, vocalized textual extracts concentrates on Old Testament nouns and verbs. Prepositions, particles, interjections, and numerals—words lacking "significant content"—are given without full references.

**232** S. E. Loewenstamm (ed.). *Thesaurus of the Language of the Bible*. Jerusalem: Bible Concordance, 1957– .

So far this useful combination of a concordance and lexicon covers the first nine letters of the Hebrew alphabet. The work gives verbs from the Masoretic Text under their roots; other words appear in the order of their initial letter.

**233** E. Hatch and H. A. Redpath. *A Concordance to the Septuagint and the Other Greek Versions of the Old Testament*.

3 vols. Oxford: Clarendon, 1897–1906. Reprinted Grand Rapids: Baker, 1983. [E. Camilo Dos Santos. *An Expanded Hebrew Index for the Hatch-Redpath "Concordance to the Septuagint."* Jerusalem: Dugith, 1974.]

This standard work on the entire Septuagint—including the apocrypha/deuterocanonicals—gives the Hebrew (or Aramaic) word or words that a particular Greek term was used to translate, where such equivalence exists. Proper names are separately presented.

**234** G. V. Wigram. *The Englishman's Hebrew and Chaldee Concordance of the Old Testament.* 5th ed. London: Bagster, 1890. Reprinted *The New Englishman's Hebrew Concordance.* Peabody: Hendrickson, 1984.

The author presents in alphabetical order every Hebrew and Aramaic term that appears in the Masoretic Text but with an English quotation of the contexts. The English rendering of each key word is italicized for easy recognition.

**235** G. Morrish. *Concordance of the Septuagint.* London: Bagster, 1887. Reprinted Grand Rapids: Zondervan, 1976.

While this handy and compact concordance omits contextual quotations as well as cross-references to Hebrew and Aramaic words, it does list every Scripture verse for each Greek term (except proper names) in the Septuagint.

**236** B. Davidson. *A Concordance of the Hebrew and Chaldee Scriptures.* Rev. ed. London: Bagster, 1876.

With Hebrew and Aramaic terms integrated into a single alphabetical list, this concordance systematically arranges all the Old Testament passages under each part of speech according to its various inflectional forms.

### 3.3 Grammars

This section mentions principally intermediate and advanced grammars. Elementary grammars appear whenever they have some sort of guidebook available. Special issues (especially the Hebrew verb) are addressed in a number of volumes. Besides Hebrew, the languages covered comprise Aramaic and Greek.

**237**   E. Ben Zvi, M. Hancock, and R. Beinert. *Readings in Biblical Hebrew: An Intermediate Textbook.* Yale Language Series. New Haven: Yale University, 1993.

This book (with a text-plus-workbook format) leads the student beyond a rudimentary knowledge of biblical Hebrew by means of direct encounter with a wide range of Old Testament passages.

**238**   W. Johnstone, I. McCafferty, and J. D. Martin. *Computerised Introductory Hebrew Grammar.* Edinburgh: Clark, 1993.

This program's interactive character, including its use of digitally recorded sound and automatically corrected exercises, requires no computer skills beyond keyboard operation.

**239**   J. L. Malone. *Tiberian Hebrew Phonology.* Winona Lake, Ind.: Eisenbrauns, 1993.

The writer describes the grammatical system of the Masoretes in light of both recent linguistic study (generative phonology) and his own far-reaching work on other Semitic languages.

**240**   J. D. Martin. *Davidson's Introductory Hebrew Grammar.* 27th ed. Edinburgh: Clark, 1993.

Within a single semester students can master this simplified grammar, which retains a sound "traditional" approach to the study of biblical Hebrew. The grammar from Johnstone and others (#238) incorporates a key to this book's exercises.

**241**   W. R. Bodine (ed.). *Linguistics and Biblical Hebrew.* Winona Lake, Ind.: Eisenbrauns, 1992.

For both students and teachers of the Hebrew language this volume introduces major kinds of linguistic analysis and samples of how each might be carried out in the Old Testament.

**242**   D. N. Freedman, A. D. Forbes, and F. I. Andersen (eds.). *Studies in Hebrew and Aramaic Orthography.* Biblical and Judaic Studies 2. Winona Lake, Ind.: Eisenbrauns, 1992.

This book summarizes the use of vowel letters in Hebrew and Aramaic, discusses the dating of the phases of Hebrew, deals with spelling in parallel passages in the Bible, and introduces alternative methods of statistical analysis.

**243** E. Simon, I. Resnikoff, and L. Motzkin. *The First Hebrew Primer: The Adult Beginner's Path to Biblical Hebrew.* 3d ed. Oakland: EKS, 1992.

A complete course of thirty lessons presents vocabulary, grammar, exercises, charts, and other devices to help students learn this ancient language. Both a Teacher's Guide and an Answer Book are available.

**244** P. Joüon. *A Grammar of Biblical Hebrew.* Revised by T. Muraoka. Subsidia Biblica 14. Rome: Biblical Institute, 1991.

A reference grammar, this tome takes into full account the advances of knowledge made in the fields of Hebrew (both biblical and postbiblical) and its cognate languages (especially the Northwest Semitic ones).

**245** A. Niccacci. *The Syntax of the Verb in Classical Hebrew Prose.* Translated by W. G. E. Watson. JSOTSup 86. Sheffield: JSOT, 1990. Original title: *Sintassi del verbo ebraico nella prosa biblica classica.* Jerusalem: Franciscan, 1986.

To the problem of the Hebrew verb, the author applies the approach of text linguistics, which studies verbal forms not in isolation but in connection with their actual textual function.

**246** J. D. Price. *The Syntax of Masoretic Accents in the Hebrew Bible.* Studies in the Bible and Early Christianity 27. Lewiston, N.Y.: Mellen, 1990.

The author supplies a formal syntax for the utilization of Hebrew accents and defines the grammar for each accent as it functions within the domain of a verse.

**247** B. K. Waltke and M. O'Connor. *An Introduction to Biblical Hebrew Syntax.* Winona Lake, Ind.: Eisenbrauns, 1990.

Some thirty-five hundred examples illustrate the points discussed in this magnificently done, modern linguistic study.

**248** J. Barr. *The Variable Spellings of the Hebrew Bible.* Oxford: Oxford University, 1989.

This book looks at and tries to make some sense of spelling differences that occur where certain vowels may or may not be spelled with vowel letters.

**249** C. L. Seow. *A Grammar for Biblical Hebrew*. Nashville: Abingdon, 1987. [J. M. Hamilton and J. S. Rogers. *"A Grammar for Biblical Hebrew" Handbook: Answer Keys and Study Guide*. Nashville: Abingdon, 1989.]

This textbook introduces the fundamentals of Hebrew grammar and consistently explains grammatical forms in terms of historical developments.

**250** F. I. Andersen and A. D. Forbes. *Spelling in the Hebrew Bible*. Biblica et Orientalia 41. Rome: Biblical Institute, 1986.

The authors describe the orthographic phenomena of the Hebrew Bible, assess the evidence by means of appropriate statistical analyses, and interpret the evidence in terms of the history of Hebrew spelling.

**251** T. Muraoka. *Emphatic Words and Structures in Biblical Hebrew*. Jerusalem: Magnes/Leiden: Brill, 1985.

The writer critically observes the means of linguistic emphasis on both the syntactic level (word order) and the lexical level (individual elements—pronouns, infinitives, and especially particles).

**252** M. Mansoor. *Biblical Hebrew Step by Step*. 3d ed. 2 vols. Grand Rapids: Baker, 1984.

Lessons include vocabulary lists, explanatory notes, translation exercises, and study hints. For each volume both a key to exercises and an audiocassette of Hebrew pronunciation are available separately.

**253** L. McFall. *The Enigma of the Hebrew Verbal System: Solutions from Ewald to the Present Day*. Historic Texts and Interpreters in Biblical Scholarship 2. Sheffield: Almond, 1982.

The author really reviews the literature on the subject starting with the earliest medieval Jewish grammarians, but he does neglect several important analyses from this century.

**254** S. B. J. Mandel. "The Development of Samaritan Hebrew: A Historical Linguistic View." Ph.D. diss., Harvard University, 1977.

> By studying the nominal patterns (extensively) and verbal patterns (sketchily) of Samaritan Hebrew, the author sizes up its contribution to our knowledge of Hebrew as a whole.

**255** J. Blau. *A Grammar of Biblical Hebrew*. Porta Linguarum Orientalium, n.s. 12. Wiesbaden: Harrassowitz, 1976.

> Both beginning and intermediate students can employ this book, which contains elementary exercises and biblical excerpts for practice as well as reasoned elucidations of more advanced problems in Hebrew grammar.

**256** J. H. Eaton (ed.). *Readings in Biblical Hebrew*. 2 vols. University Semitics Study Aids 3–4. Birmingham: University of Birmingham, 1976–78.

> The contributors have aimed to guide those who are not yet veterans at reading the Hebrew Bible toward both grammatical understanding and aesthetic appreciation of all sorts of scriptural passages.

**257** T. W. Nakarai. *Biblical Hebrew*. Rev. ed. Johnson City: Emmanuel School of Religion, 1976.

> This book forthrightly states the facts of the language and effectively illustrates each principle enunciated. Nearly one-third of the grammar deals with syntax.

**258** R. J. Williams. *Hebrew Syntax: An Outline*. 2d ed. Toronto: University of Toronto, 1976.

> Emphasizing the significance of word order in Hebrew, the author quotes abundantly from the Old Testament to illuminate the syntax of nouns, verbs, particles, and clauses.

**259** F. I. Andersen. *The Sentence in Biblical Hebrew*. Janua Linguarum, Series Practica 231. Hague: Mouton, 1974.

> Basing his research upon advances in linguistic theory and method, the writer has conducted a fresh and thorough examination of the sentence system of ancient Hebrew.

**260** A. F. Johns. *A Short Grammar of Biblical Aramaic*. Rev. ed. Andrews University Monographs 1. Berrien Springs, Mich.: Andrews University, 1972.

> The author organizes the material for sessions in the classroom (with graduated vocabulary assignments and Aramaic-to-English exercises) and assumes student acquaintance with biblical Hebrew.

**261** T. O. Lambdin. *Introduction to Biblical Hebrew*. New York: Scribner's, 1971. London: Darton, 1973. [H. G. M. Williamson. *Annotated Key to Lambdin's "Introduction to Biblical Hebrew."* JSOT Manuals 3. Sheffield: JSOT, 1987.]

> This philologically up-to-date work is perhaps the most sophisticated of the elementary grammars.

**262** A. Sperber. *A Historical Grammar of Biblical Hebrew: A Presentation of Problems with Suggestions to Their Solution*. Leiden: Brill, 1966.

> The author diligently analyzes a wide collection of instances of grammatical features from throughout the Old Testament.

**263** O. L. Barnes. *A New Approach to the Problem of the Hebrew Tenses*. Oxford: Thornton, 1965.

> The writer advocates an explanation for Hebrew verb usage that sees the time of a situation as being located relative to the time of the preceding verb.

**264** A. Murtonen. *A Grammar of the Samaritan Dialect of Hebrew*. Studia Orientalia 29. Vol. 3 of *Materials for a Non-Masoretic Hebrew Grammar*. Helsinki: Finnish Oriental Society, 1964.

> This book's first (and longer) part on phonology and morphology is purely diachronic while the second part on (mostly sentential) syntax is based on essentially synchronic material.

**265** J. W. Watts. *A Survey of Syntax in the Hebrew Old Testament*. Rev. ed. Grand Rapids: Eerdmans, 1964.

> The writer's treatment of syntactical constructions in simple, compound, and complex sentences pays special attention to features of the Hebrew verb.

**266** F. Rosenthal. *A Grammar of Biblical Aramaic*. Porta Linguarum Orientalium, n.s. 5. Wiesbaden: Harrassowitz, 1961.

In this slender but very reliable volume, the writer provides beginners with the elements of the language. G. H. Wilson (*Journal of Semitic Studies* 24 [1979]: 21–24) has prepared an index to scriptural passages quoted.

**267** A. Sperber. *A Grammar of Masoretic Hebrew*. Copenhagen: Munksgaard, 1959.

This guide to an understanding of principally four manuscripts being regarded as the "pre-Masoretic Bible" records novel views about Hebrew grammar (especially phonology).

**268** J. Weingreen. *Classical Hebrew Composition*. Oxford: Clarendon, 1957.

The English exercises and notes are designed to produce (through a systematic presentation of the pattern of Old Testament language) an understanding of the modes of Hebrew thinking and expression.

**269** H. W. Smyth. *Greek Grammar*. Revised by G. M. Messing. Cambridge: Harvard University, 1956. [W. A. Schumann (comp.). *Index of Passages Cited in Herbert Weir Smyth, "Greek Grammar."* Scholarly Aids 1. Watertown, Mass.: Eaton, 1961.]

This, the most complete descriptive grammar of ancient Greek to appear in English, offers insight into the language of the Septuagint.

**270** F. R. Blake. *A Resurvey of Hebrew Tenses*. Scripta Pontificii Instituti Biblici 103. Rome: Biblical Institute, 1951. Reprinted Graz: Akademische, 1968.

The author opposes the theory (championed by Samuel Driver, #280) that Hebrew verbs expressed type of action rather than time of action.

**271** G. D. Young. *Grammar of the Hebrew Language*. Grand Rapids: Zondervan, 1951.

This volume, whose second part describes the language found in the Hebrew Bible, features diagnostic tools for the exact identification of verb forms.

**272**  G. R. Driver. *Problems of the Hebrew Verbal System.* Old
Testament Studies 2. Edinburgh: Clark, 1936.

Because the author concluded that Hebrew was an amal-
gam of several languages, he judged the Hebrew verbal
system to be similarly a conflation of more than one system.

**273**  W. W. Goodwin. *Greek Grammar.* Revised by C. B. Gulick.
Boston: Ginn, 1930.

Septuagintal scholars can benefit from this very thorough
explanation of the Greek language as found mainly in the
classical literature.

**274**  H. Bauer and P. Leander. *Historische Grammatik der hebräischen Sprache des Alten Testaments.* Halle: Niemeyer,
1922. Reprinted Hildesheim, Germany: Olms, 1962.

Though dated, many aspects of this massive volume on
biblical Hebrew orthography, phonology, and morphol-
ogy can still be used—especially the classes of verbs and
nouns.

**275**  G. Bergsträsser. *Hebräische Grammatik.* 29th ed. 2 vols.
Leipzig: Vogel, 1918. Hinrichs, 1929. Reprinted Hildesheim,
Germany: Olms, 1962. [L. G. Running. *Hebräisches Wort-
register zur "Hebräischen Grammatik" von G. Bergsträsser.* Hildesheim, Germany: Olms, 1968.]

An improvement over the previous edition of the grammar by Wilhelm Gesenius, this unfinished reference
work, however, covers only orthography and phonology
in its first part and verbs in its second.

**276**  A. E. Cowley (ed.). *Gesenius' Hebrew Grammar.* 2d ed. Oxford: Clarendon, 1910.

This comprehensive survey, with extensive textual citations, easily remained the best biblical Hebrew reference
grammar in English until the recent appearance of
Joüon's revised grammar in English dress (#244).

**277**  H. S. J. Thackeray. *A Grammar of the Old Testament in
Greek.* Cambridge: Cambridge University, 1909.

Even though its coverage is limited mainly to morphol-
ogy, this work continues to be an indispensable grammar
for the Septuagint.

**278** F. C. Conybeare and S. G. Stock. *Selections from the Septuagint*. Boston: Ginn, 1905. Reprinted *Grammar of Septuagint Greek*. Peabody: Hendrickson, 1988.

Designed for the beginner in Septuagintal studies, this standard discussion of Greek grammar presents it in a careful and succinct way.

**279** A. B. Davidson. *Hebrew Syntax*. 3d ed. Edinburgh: Clark, 1901.

The writer's treatment of the main principles of syntax for the pronoun, noun, verb, and sentence is printed in larger type while treatment of the less common usages is thrown into the form of notes.

**280** S. R. Driver. *A Treatise on the Use of the Tenses in Hebrew*. 3d ed. Oxford: Clarendon, 1892.

This analysis, in which the author emphasizes that the Hebrew verbal system does not primarily concern time relations, stands out as a classic on the subject.

# 4

## Cognate Literature

### 4.1 Jewish Writings

The works contained here offer English translations of ancient Israelite and Jewish documents like Qumran manuscripts, the pseudepigrapha, inscriptions from Egypt and Palestine, and the writings of Philo and Josephus. Several introductions to these materials are cited, too.

**281** F. García Martínez. *The Dead Sea Scrolls Translated: The Qumran Texts in English*. Leiden: Brill, 1994.

> This carefully edited work presents the largest collection of Dead Sea Scrolls ever published in English. The book concludes with an exhaustive list of all manuscripts discovered at Qumran.

**282** J. C. VanderKam. *The Dead Sea Scrolls Today*. Grand Rapids: Eerdmans, 1994.

> Pictures supplement the text of this up-to-date guide to all the Scrolls—both published and unpublished. It discusses what the scrolls tell us about the community associated with them and what importance they hold for biblical studies.

**283** J. H. Charlesworth (ed.). *The Dead Sea Scrolls*. 10 vols. Louisville: Westminster/Tübingen: Mohr, 1993– .

Participating scholars will introduce, transliterate, translate, and annotate every sectarian Qumran text currently known.

**284** R. H. Eisenman and M. Wise (eds.). *The Dead Sea Scrolls Uncovered: The First Complete Translation and Interpretation of 50 Key Documents Withheld for over 35 Years.* Shaftesbury, England: Element, 1992. Reprinted New York: Penguin, 1993.

The texts that are given here—in Hebrew transcription and English translation for both scholars and laypersons—exhibit messianism, divination, astrology, mystery, prophecy, ecstasy, myth, and more.

**285** W. A. Horbury and D. Noy (eds.). *Jewish Inscriptions of Graeco-Roman Egypt.* Cambridge: Cambridge University, 1992.

This book collects, translates, comments upon, and indexes all known Jewish inscriptions from Egypt between the third century B.C. and the sixth century A.D.

**286** K. A. D. Smelik. *Writings from Ancient Israel: A Handbook of Historical and Religious Documents.* Translated by G. I. Davies. Louisville: Westminster/Edinburgh: Clark, 1992. Original title: *Behouden schrift.* Baarn, Netherlands: Ten Have, 1984.

In a readable and up-to-date resource, the editor has translated a compilation of important and fascinating remnants of early Hebrew inscriptions and interpreted them in light of their historical, social, and biblical contexts.

**287** M. A. Knibb. *The Qumran Community.* Cambridge Commentaries on Writings of the Jewish and Christian World 2. Cambridge: Cambridge University, 1987.

This study presents portions from the literary materials found in the caves at the site of Qumran. For each selection there is a general introduction, outline, brief bibliography, translation, and commentary.

**288** G. Vermes. *The Dead Sea Scrolls in English.* 3d ed. Harmondsworth, England: Penguin, 1987.

While a most comprehensive single-volume English translation, it is less than easy to consult since the editor does not number the lines of these nonbiblical scrolls. Three very reliable chapters on the Qumran community precede the texts themselves.

**289** B. Porten and A. Yardeni (eds.). *Textbook of Aramaic Documents from Ancient Egypt.* Texts and Studies for Students. Jerusalem: Hebrew University, 1986– .

Supplied with wonderful facsimiles, this excellent English translation of Aramaic letters, contracts, lists, inscriptions, and the like, is based on a new reading of the originals.

**290** M. de Jonge (ed.). *Outside the Old Testament.* Cambridge Commentaries on Writings of the Jewish and Christian World 4. Cambridge: Cambridge University, 1985.

This modest work brings together fascinating extracts from twelve pseudepigraphous writings as well as introductions to them by specialists in the field.

**291** W. Barnstone (ed.). *The Other Bible.* San Francisco: Harper, 1984.

The editor has collected English translations of ancient, esoteric texts that came out of both the Jewish and Christian traditions, but which were shut out from the official canons of the Old and New Testaments.

**292** H. F. D. Sparks (ed.). *The Apocryphal Old Testament.* Oxford: Clarendon, 1984.

The English translation of twenty-five pseudepigraphal writings has been produced afresh and fitted out with short introductions and bibliographies.

**293** M. E. Stone (ed.). *Jewish Writings of the Second Temple Period: Apocrypha, Pseudepigrapha, Qumran Sectarian Writings, Philo, Josephus.* Philadelphia: Fortress/Assen, Netherlands: Van Gorcum, 1984.

This tome may serve as a nearly exhaustive introduction to the literary production of Judaism in the period of the Second Temple—excluding the Hebrew Old Testament on the one hand and rabbinic literature on the other.

**294** J. H. Charlesworth (ed.). *The Old Testament Pseude-pigrapha*. 2 vols. Garden City, N.Y.: Doubleday/London: Darton, 1983–85.

The English translations for this collection of pseude-pigraphous documents have been freshly made from the best available critical texts.

**295** M. Mansoor. *The Dead Sea Scrolls: A Textbook and Study Guide*. 2d ed. Grand Rapids: Baker, 1983.

In outline form for a nontechnical audience, the author gives a trustworthy assessment of the nature and meaning of the manuscripts from the Judaean desert.

**296** M. McNamara. *Intertestamental Literature*. Old Testament Message 23. Wilmington, Del.: Glazier, 1983.

With sometimes extensive excerpts sprinkled throughout, this work considers the noncanonical literature composed during the three centuries between 200 B.C. and A.D. 100.

**297** G. W. E. Nickelsburg and M. E. Stone. *Faith and Piety in Early Judaism: Texts and Documents*. Philadelphia: Fortress, 1983. Reprinted Philadelphia: Trinity, 1991.

Through background comments and explanatory notes, this anthology makes primary sources from the Second Temple period readily accessible to students and the broader public.

**298** D. Pardee. *Handbook of Ancient Hebrew Letters*. Sources for Biblical Study 15. Chico, Calif.: Scholars, 1982.

This study edition provides bibliography, consonantal text, English translation, philological notes, epistolographic considerations, and general interpretation for each of four dozen letters dating from the seventh century B.C. to the second century A.D.

**299** Y. Aharoni and A. F. Rainey. *Arad Inscriptions*. Rev. ed. Judean Desert Studies. Jerusalem: Israel Exploration Society, 1981.

This critical edition presents well over one hundred Hebrew and Aramaic inscriptions from Tel Arad by means of photographs, English translations, and commentaries.

**300** H. W. Attridge and R. A. Oden, Jr. *Philo of Byblos: The Phoenician History.* Catholic Biblical Quarterly Monograph Series 9. Washington: Catholic Biblical Association, 1981.

> An introduction and notes accompany a critical text and an English translation of the Phoenician History, which has numerous points of contact with the Bible.

**301** G. W. E. Nickelsburg. *Jewish Literature between the Bible and the Mishnah: A Historical and Literary Introduction.* Philadelphia: Fortress/London; SCM, 1981.

> This valuable resource systematically seeks to relate the literature to the historical periods in which it took shape and attempts to show how the various Jewish writers faced the problems of their age.

**302** S. Sandmel. *Philo of Alexandria: An Introduction.* New York: Oxford University, 1979.

> This work, written for beginners in the study of Philo, first discusses Philo's thought and then his relation to Palestinian Judaism, gnosticism, and Christianity.

**303** J. A. Fitzmyer and D. J. Harrington. *A Manual of Palestinian Aramaic Texts (Second Century B.C.– Second Century A.D.).* Biblica et Orientalia 34. Rome: Biblical Institute, 1978.

> The editors provide these (frequently fragmentary) inscriptions with English translations, brief descriptive notes, glossaries, and a secondary bibliography.

**304** T. H. Gaster. *The Dead Sea Scriptures.* 3d ed. Garden City, N.Y.: Doubleday, 1976.

> One of the better English translations of the major Dead Sea Scrolls is found here, along with an introduction and notes.

**305** B. Jongeling, C. J. Labuschagne, and A. S. van der Woude. *Aramaic Texts from Qumran.* Semitic Study Series, n.s. 4. Leiden: Brill, 1976.

> The writers designed the book especially for those who are not specialists in the field of Dead Sea Scrolls study. English translations face the texts, which are detailedly introduced and extensively annotated.

**306**  *Inscriptions Reveal: Documents from the Time of the Bible, the Mishna, and the Talmud.* Jerusalem: Israel Museum, 1972.

Accurate translations and explanations of ancient Hebrew inscriptions accompany good reproductions of a large number of the originals.

**307**  R. A. Kraft (ed.). Society of Biblical Literature Texts and Translations, Pseudepigrapha Series. Atlanta: Scholars, 1972– .

This series embraces volumes on such pseudepigraphic "intertestamental" literature as the Testament of Abraham, the Odes of Solomon, the History of the Rechabites, the Apocalypse of Elijah, and the Book of Mysteries.

**308**  J. M. Allegro. *The Dead Sea Scrolls: A Reappraisal.* 2d ed. Baltimore: Penguin, 1964.

This discussion of the Dead Sea Scrolls incorporates partial translations of the Manual of Discipline and the Thanksgiving Hymns among others.

**309**  E. R. Goodenough. *An Introduction to Philo Judaeus.* 2d ed. Oxford: Blackwell, 1962. New York: Barnes, 1963. Reprinted Lanham, Md.: University Press of America, 1986.

The author has composed a valuable introduction to Philo of Alexandria: his writings, his political thinking, his Jewishness, and his metaphysics, ethics, and mysticism.

**310**  A. Dupont-Sommer. *The Essene Writings from Qumran.* Translated by G. Vermes. Cleveland: World/Oxford: Blackwell, 1961. Reprinted Gloucester, Mass.: Smith, 1973. Original title: *Les écrits esséniens découverts près de la mer Morte.* Paris: Payot, 1959.

The author has produced an extremely serviceable translation of the Dead Sea Scrolls by supplying column and line numbers, so that one can easily find a Qumran passage being sought.

**311**  R. K. Harrison. *The Dead Sea Scrolls: An Introduction.* New York: Harper, 1961.

The author surveys the Qumran manuscript discoveries and offers a substantial summary of the then present state of scholarly work on the Scrolls.

**312**  E. F. Sutcliffe. *The Monks of Qumran.* Westminster, Md.: Newman/London: Burns, 1960.

Translations of Dead Sea Scrolls constitute more than one-third of this book, which treats the people of Qumran as a religious community and investigates their history, mode of life, and beliefs.

**313**  M. Burrows. *More Light on the Dead Sea Scrolls: New Scrolls and New Interpretations.* New York: Viking/London: Secker, 1958.

The author updates his previous work (#316) and translates additional documents like the Genesis Apocryphon, the Prayer of Nabonidus, Florilegium, and the Blessings of Jacob.

**314**  H. E. del Medico. *The Riddle of the Scrolls.* Translated by H. Garner. New York: McBride/London: Burke, 1958. Original title: *L'énigme des manuscrits de la mer Morte.* Paris: Plon, 1957.

The editor studies the provenance and contents of the manuscripts discovered in Qumran Cave 1 and provides an annotated translation of the principal texts.

**315**  G. R. Driver. *Aramaic Documents of the Fifth Century B.C.* Rev. ed. Oxford: Clarendon, 1957.

For both scholars and students, the editor has published thirteen letters from the chancery of a Persian satrap of ancient Egypt. A glossary with all the terms in the documents follows the texts, English translations, and philological notes.

**316**  M. Burrows. *The Dead Sea Scrolls.* New York: Viking, 1955. London: Secker, 1956.

The editor soberly studies the Dead Sea Scrolls and translates the Damascus Document, the Commentary on Habakkuk, selections from the War Scroll, and so forth.

**317**  Discoveries in the Judaean Desert. Oxford: Clarendon, 1955– .

This important series presents the first printed editions of manuscripts from Qumran, Murabba'at, and Naḥal Ḥever. Translations often supplement transcriptions and excellent photographs.

**318**  E. G. Kraeling (ed.). *The Brooklyn Museum Aramaic Papyri.* Publications of the Department of Egyptian Art. New Haven: Yale University/London: Oxford University, 1953. Reprinted New York: Arno, 1969.

A historical introduction precedes the printing of seventeen documents from fifth-century B.C. Elephantine, their English translations, and commentaries on them. A pair of indexes (of words and proper names) and nearly two dozen plates follow.

**319**  M. Hadas (ed.). *Aristeas to Philocrates (Letter of Aristeas).* Jewish Apocryphal Literature. New York: Harper, 1951. Reprinted New York: Ktav, 1973.

This volume includes the original text and a translation into English as well as an introduction and brief notes.

**320**  F. H. Colson, G. H. Whitaker, J. W. Earp, and R. Marcus. *Philo.* 12 vols. Loeb Classical Library. Cambridge: Harvard University/London: Heinemann, 1929–62.

This set offers ready access to good Greek and Armenian texts of Philo Judaeus, an English translation with brief technical notes, and a general index.

**321**  H. S. J. Thackeray, R. Marcus, A. Wikgren, and L. H. Feldman. *Josephus.* 10 vols. Loeb Classical Library. Cambridge: Harvard University/London: Heinemann, 1926–65.

This edition supplies not only a fine Greek text of Josephus but also an English translation, short critical remarks, and an important index to the whole.

**322**  A. E. Cowley (ed.). *Aramaic Papyri of the Fifth Century B.C.* Oxford: Clarendon, 1923. Reprinted Osnabrück: Zeller, 1967.

In a single volume the compiler chronologically arranges all the legible pre-Christian Aramaic papyri known to him. The book contains the Aramaic texts, English translations, and a commentary in support of the readings and interpretations adopted.

**323**  R. H. Charles (ed.). *The Apocrypha and Pseudepigrapha of the Old Testament.* 2 vols. Oxford: Clarendon, 1913.

Volume two contains English translations of the pseudepigraphical literature as well as extensive introductions, explanatory notes, and a detailed topical index.

**324**  S. Schechter (ed.). *Documents of Jewish Sectaries.* 2 vols. Cambridge: Cambridge University, 1910. Reprinted New York: Ktav, 1970.

Volume one contains the first printed edition (along with a translation) of the Damascus Document—also called the Zadokite Fragments—that came from the Cairo Geniza.

**325**  C. D. Yonge. *The Works of Philo Judaeus, the Contemporary of Josephus.* 4 vols. London: Bohn, 1854–55. Reprinted Peabody: Hendrickson, 1993.

Both an addition of newly translated sections (previously omitted from the original volumes) and a keying of the English translation to the numbering system of the Loeb edition (#320) highlight this convenient reprint.

**326**  W. Whiston. *The Genuine Works of Flavius Josephus.* 6 vols. Worcester, Mass.: Thomas, 1794. Reprinted Peabody: Hendrickson, 1980.

This noteworthy English translation of Josephus's writings is supplemented by seven topical discussions relating to him.

## 4.2 Near Eastern Parallels

One can locate in this section both introductions to and English translations of literature from Amarna, Mesopotamia, Ugarit, Egypt, Transjordan, and Syria. Some books are collections of many ancient pieces; some take up a single, lengthy item.

**327**  B. R. Foster. *Before the Muses: An Anthology of Akkadian Literature.* 2 vols. Bethesda: CDL, 1993.

This work contains translations of over three hundred Babylonian and Assyrian compositions, along with notes on philology and references to previous treatments.

**328** W. L. Moran (ed.). *The Amarna Letters*. Baltimore: Johns Hopkins University, 1992.

> The author introduces, translates, and annotates the entire corpus of Amarna letters—taking into account the progress of scholarly understanding over the last seventy-five years.

**329** V. H. Matthews and D. C. Benjamin. *Old Testament Parallels: Laws and Stories from the Ancient Near East*. New York: Paulist, 1991.

> This illustrated classroom edition of eastern Mediterranean literature—freshly translated into English—explains how individual documents throw light on similar scriptural materials.

**330** B. Long (ed.). Writings from the Ancient World. Atlanta: Scholars, 1990– .

> For both specialists and general readers this series will introduce, transliterate, and translate ancient Near Eastern myths, law codes, letters, commercial documents, hymns, prayers, treaties, and the like.

**331** S. Dalley. *Myths from Mesopotamia: Creation, the Flood, Gilgamesh, and Others*. Oxford: Oxford University, 1989.

> A glossary (of names and terms) and a bibliography (of secondary literature) follow an accurate rendering into current English of the best-preserved Akkadian stories.

**332** M. G. Kovacs. *The Epic of Gilgamesh*. Stanford, Calif.: Stanford University, 1989.

> The author bases a new and very readable English translation on all of the copies known from antiquity. There are a few nontechnical introductory remarks.

**333** B. Margalit. *The Ugaritic Poem of AQHT: Text, Translation, Commentary*. Beiheft zur Zeitschrift für die alttestamentliche Wissenschaft 182. Berlin: de Gruyter, 1989.

> At once analytical and synthetic, this descriptive study pays attention to formal and structural elements as well as to thematic and ideological matters.

**334** P. Michalowski (ed.). *The Lamentation over the Destruction of Sumer and Ur.* Mesopotamian Civilizations 1. Winona Lake, Ind.: Eisenbrauns, 1989.

Along with an introduction and indexes, this work presents the entirety of the long Sumerian poem describing the suffering in Babylonia during the final days of Ur's Third Dynasty.

**335** J. H. Walton. *Ancient Israelite Literature in Its Cultural Context: A Survey of Parallels between Biblical and Ancient Near Eastern Texts.* Library of Biblical Interpretation. Grand Rapids: Zondervan, 1989.

Within various literary genres (such as cosmology and prophecy), the author surveys parallels between the Old Testament and other ancient Near Eastern texts.

**336** T. Jacobsen (ed.). *The Harps That Once . . . : Sumerian Poetry in Translation.* New Haven: Yale University, 1987.

The writer concentrates on myths, epics, hymns, and laments from the Old Babylonian period. He has kept his annotated translation as literal as possible.

**337** R. O. Faulkner (trans.). *The Ancient Egyptian Book of the Dead.* Edited by C. Andrews. Rev. ed. New York: Macmillan/London: British Museum, 1985. Reprinted Austin: University of Texas, 1990.

Illustrated with sixty color and eighty-five black-and-white vignettes, this standard volume expertly translates a funerary collection of religious and magical texts.

**338** J. A. Hackett. *The Balaam Text from Deir ʿAllā.* Harvard Semitic Monographs 31. Chico, Calif.: Scholars, 1984.

The heart of this slender book transliterates, translates, and analyzes the text, but its grammar (including script) is also looked at in much detail.

**339** J. O'Brien and W. Major. *In the Beginning: Creation Myths from Ancient Mesopotamia, Israel, and Greece.* American Academy of Religion Aids for the Study of Religion 11. Chico, Calif.: Scholars, 1982.

These fresh contemporary translations with study questions allow students to encounter both universal patterns and distinctive traits in the creation myths of the three cultures chosen.

340  G. Pettinato. *The Archives of Ebla: An Empire Inscribed in Clay.* Garden City, N.Y.: Doubleday, 1981. Original title: *Ebla.* Milan: Mondadori, 1979.

In this popular account of the discovery of Eblaite and its significance for the study of the Old Testament are quite a few texts in English translation.

341  W. Beyerlin (ed.). *Near Eastern Religious Texts Relating to the Old Testament.* Translated by J. Bowden. Philadelphia: Westminster/London: SCM, 1978. Original title: *Religionsgeschichtliches Textbuch zum Alten Testament.* Göttingen: Vandenhoeck, 1985.

This thorough selection of ancient Egyptian, Mesopotamian, Hittite, Ugaritic, and northwestern Semitic documents in English translation comes with comprehensive introductions and helpful notes.

342  M. D. Coogan. *Stories from Ancient Canaan.* Philadelphia: Westminster, 1978.

In this excellent and readable English translation, the author presents three major story cycles and a pair of short mythological writings from Ugarit.

343  J. C. L. Gibson. *Canaanite Myths and Legends.* Edinburgh: Clark, 1977.

Actually a revision of the work by Driver (#359), this book publishes a usable and reliable transliteration, English translation, textual commentary, and bibliography for Ugaritic stories.

344  J. Hoftijzer and G. van der Kooij (eds.). *Aramaic Texts from Deir 'Alla.* Documenta et Monumenta Orientis Antiqui 19. Leiden: Brill, 1976.

This first printed edition of the texts contains their transcription, an English translation of them, an extensive and ingenious philological commentary, and an assemblage of plates.

**345** R. O. Faulkner. *The Ancient Egyptian Coffin Texts.* 3 vols. Modern Egyptology Series. Warminster, England: Aris, 1973–78.

The author has produced a superior rendering of these religious and mythological documents into English. Commentary on the spells is confined mostly to textual and philological matters.

**346** M. Lichtheim. *Ancient Egyptian Literature: A Book of Readings.* 3 vols. Berkeley: University of California, 1973–80.

Arranged chronologically and topically, a representative selection of compositions written on either papyrus or stone is translated and annotated in these convenient and modern volumes.

**347** W. K. Simpson (ed.). *The Literature of Ancient Egypt: An Anthology of Stories, Instructions, and Poetry.* New ed. New Haven: Yale University, 1973.

The editor has brought together a number of compositions, which are grouped by genre, rendered into contemporary English, and provided with short introductions.

**348** L. R. Fisher and S. Rummel (eds.). *Ras Shamra Parallels: The Texts from Ugarit and the Hebrew Bible.* 3 vols. Analecta Orientalia 49–51. Rome: Biblical Institute, 1972–81.

This very useful collection is built around terms and concepts occurring in both Ugaritic and Hebrew. Each entry has a translated Ugaritic passage, textual notes, and bibliography.

**349** N. K. Sandars. *The Epic of Gilgamesh.* Rev. ed. Harmondsworth, England: Penguin, 1972.

An extensive introduction precedes this fine English version of the cycle of poems collected around the character of Gilgamesh. A glossary and a bibliography follow.

**350** J. C. L. Gibson. *Textbook of Syrian Semitic Inscriptions.* 3 vols. Oxford: Clarendon, 1971–82.

This fine analytical collection of Hebrew, Moabite, Aramaic, and Phoenician inscriptions—translated into English—is a valuable resource for understanding the Old Testament.

**351** N. K. Sandars (trans.). *Poems of Heaven and Hell from Ancient Mesopotamia.* Harmondsworth, England: Penguin, 1971.

In this volume, five hymns and tales dating from the height of Babylonian civilization in the second millennium B.C. receive straightforward English renderings.

**352** R. O. Faulkner. *The Ancient Egyptian Pyramid Texts.* Oxford: Clarendon, 1969. Reprinted Oak Park: Bolchazy/Warminster, England: Aris, 1985.

The author provides a good English translation for these literary remains inscribed on tomb monuments at Saqqara during the reigns of Egyptian monarchs in Dynasties V-VII.

**353** W. G. Lambert and A. R. Millard. *Atra-ḫasīs: The Babylonian Story of the Flood.* Oxford: Clarendon, 1969.

This critical edition includes a transliteration and an English translation of the epic. The introduction was penned with the needs of those who are not cuneiform scholars in view.

**354** J. B. Pritchard (ed.). *Ancient Near Eastern Texts Relating to the Old Testament.* 3d ed. Princeton: Princeton University, 1969.

Experts in Egyptian, Sumerian, Akkadian, Hittite, Ugaritic, South Arabic, Canaanite, and Aramaic have masterfully translated primary sources for the nonspecialist. Among the indexes is one of biblical references.

**355** T. H. Gaster. *Thespis: Ritual, Myth, and Drama in the Ancient Near East.* New ed. Garden City, N.Y.: Doubleday, 1961. Reprinted New York: Gordian, 1975.

Most of this erudite book consists of English translations and interpretations of Ugaritic, Hittite, and Egyptian texts along with philological and archaeological notes.

**356** W. G. Lambert. *Babylonian Wisdom Literature.* Oxford: Clarendon, 1960.

The writer has amassed and accurately translated into English the major Babylonian texts that relate to the biblical wisdom books such as Job, Proverbs, and Ecclesiastes.

**357** J. B. Pritchard (ed.). *The Ancient Near East.* 2 vols. Princeton: Princeton University, 1958–75.

> English translations of ancient texts together with pictures of sites, statues, and artifacts shed much light on history, life, and events in the Old Testament era.

**358** D. W. Thomas (ed.). *Documents from Old Testament Times.* London: Nelson, 1958. Reprinted New York: Harper, 1961.

> The British and Canadian scholars involved added excellent introductions and notes to their English translations of Akkadian, Egyptian, Moabite, Hebrew, and Aramaic writings.

**359** G. R. Driver. *Canaanite Myths and Legends.* Old Testament Studies 3. Edinburgh: Clark, 1956.

> The writer gives a transliteration and English translation of the poems, and supplements them with observations on philology and grammar as well as with a Ugaritic glossary.

**360** S. A. B. Mercer. *The Pyramid Texts.* 4 vols. New York: Longmans, 1952.

> This work aims to furnish in English translation and with commentary the ancient Egyptian myths, rituals, hymns, prayers, and the like inscribed on limestone in the tombs.

**361** A. Heidel. *The Babylonian Genesis: The Story of the Creation.* 2d ed. Chicago: University of Chicago, 1951.

> A brief introduction dealing with such matters as the provenance and purpose of each creation account precedes a complete translation of the various cuneiform tablets from Mesopotamia.

**362** C. H. Gordon. *Ugaritic Literature: A Comprehensive Translation of the Poetic and Prose Texts.* Scripta Pontificii Instituti Biblici 98. Rome: Biblical Institute, 1949.

> The writer supplies English translations for epistles, diplomatic and administrative texts, hippic prescriptions, and inventories in addition to myths and legends.

**363** A. Heidel. *The Gilgamesh Epic and Old Testament Parallels.* 2d ed. Chicago: University of Chicago, 1949.

This book is intended for a wide circle of readers. Hence, the Akkadian texts are offered in English translation only and discussion is confined chiefly to matters of general interest.

**364** A. Erman. *The Literature of the Ancient Egyptians: Poems, Narratives, and Manuals of Instruction.* Translated by A. M. Blackman. New York: Dutton/London: Methuen, 1927. Reprinted New York: Arno, 1977. Original title: *Die Literatur der Aegypter.* Leipzig: Hinrich, 1923.

Explanatory notes on religion, history, and geography accompany the English translation, which sets out to acquaint students with texts assembled from the third and second millenia B.C.

**365** D. D. Luckenbill. *Ancient Records of Assyria and Babylonia.* 2 vols. Ancient Records. Chicago: University of Chicago, 1926–27. Reprinted London: Histories, 1989.

Based on a collation of published texts with their originals, this English version represents the historical records of just Assyria from the earliest times to the fall of Nineveh.

**366** J. H. Breasted (ed.). *Ancient Records of Egypt: Historical Documents.* 5 vols. Ancient Records. Chicago: University of Chicago, 1906–07. Reprinted London: Histories, 1988.

As literally as possible without wrenching English idiom, the author has translated sources from the beginnings of the nation until the advent of the Persians in 525 B.C.

# 5

# The Environment

## 5.1 Archaeology

Most of the following works are general but a few constitute focused studies. Ancient Palestine is the region receiving the greatest attention. Several volumes treat what might be called "culture," that is, Israel's institutions and social world.

**367** V. Fritz. *An Introduction to Biblical Archaeology.* JSOTSup 172. Sheffield: JSOT, 1993.

> This guide for scholars and students covers the physical geography and archaeologically attested history of the Holy Land in addition to a recounting of the excavation of Palestine.

**368** E. Stern (ed.). *The New Encyclopedia of Archaeological Excavations in the Holy Land.* 4 vols. New York: Simon/Jerusalem: Carta, 1993.

> This update of a classic reference enables every serious student of the Holy Land to enjoy the fruits of the many-faceted research assembled over the years by scholars—their conclusions, achievements, problems, and doubts.

**369** A. Ben-Tor (ed.). *The Archaeology of Ancient Israel.* Translated by R. Greenberg. New Haven: Yale University, 1992. Original title: *Archaeology of Ancient Israel in the Biblical Period* (in Hebrew). Tel Aviv: Open University, 1989.

In this lavishly illustrated and well-organized book, some of Israel's foremost archaeologists present a thorough introduction to early life in the Holy Land between the eighth millennium and the sixth century B.C.

**370** J. P. Free. *Archaeology and Bible History.* Updated by H. F. Vos. Rev. ed. Grand Rapids: Zondervan, 1992.

In that its writers have used Bible history as the unifying element rather than a topical approach, this book differs from others on biblical archaeology.

**371** W. E. Rast. *Through the Ages in Palestinian Archaeology: An Introductory Handbook.* Philadelphia: Trinity, 1992.

This reference—written in a lively and engaging style—combines prehistoric, biblical, and later evidence from both Israel and Jordan. The author provides readers with explanations of terms, geographical locations, dates, archaeological procedures, and scriptural links.

**372** V. H. Matthews. *Manners and Customs in the Bible.* Rev. ed. Peabody: Hendrickson, 1991.

Each chapter of this guide focuses on one period in Israel's history and shows how selected scenes from Scripture (as well as material from extrabiblical sources) throw light on the life of the people at that time.

**373** P. R. S. Moorey. *A Century of Biblical Archaeology.* Cambridge, England: Lutterworth, 1991. Louisville: Westminster, 1992.

With accurate reporting and sound evaluations, the author reviews the work of major excavators and scholars, gives the names and dates of digs, and highlights findings.

**374** W. G. Dever. *Recent Archaeological Discoveries and Biblical Research.* Seattle: University of Washington, 1990.

This work aims to acquaint the layperson who is interested in Scripture with some of the latest methods and results of archaeology in Israel as well as to stimulate dialogue between archaeologists and biblicists.

**375** A. Mazar. *Archaeology of the Land of the Bible, 10,000–586 B.C.E.* Anchor Bible Reference Library. New York: Doubleday, 1990.

This is a complete and scholarly introduction to biblical archaeology—from the very beginnings to the divided kingdoms of Israel and Judah.

376  A. Negev (ed.). *The Archaeological Encyclopedia of the Holy Land*. 3d ed. New York: Prentice, 1990.

This encyclopedia intersperses several general articles among those describing excavations carried out at or near the majority of places named in the Bible.

377  R. Gower. *The New Manners and Customs of Bible Times*. Chicago: Moody, 1987.

In this book about the individual, the family, and institutions, the author has sought to give readers a feel for biblical times so that the whole Bible would come more alive.

378  K. M. Kenyon. *The Bible and Recent Archaeology*. Revised by P. R. S. Moorey. New ed. Atlanta: Knox/London: British Museum, 1987.

In this classic work on the relationship between archaeology and Scripture, the writers discuss discoveries touching on such subjects as the patriarchs, the divided monarchy, and the nascent Church.

379  H. O. Thompson. *Biblical Archaeology: The World, the Mediterranean, the Bible*. New York: Paragon, 1987.

The writer describes the development of archaeology in general and records an abundance of cases in which archaeological discovery sheds light on the Bible.

380  T. Dowley (ed.). *Discovering the Bible: Archaeologists Look at Scripture*. Grand Rapids: Eerdmans/Basingstoke, England: Pickering, 1986.

This masterfully planned and executed resource by practicing archaeologists about recent finds that illuminate events in the biblical era is packed with pictures, maps, and charts.

381  J. A. Thompson. *Handbook of Life in Bible Times*. Leicester: Inter-Varsity, 1986.

With beautiful pictures, maps, and charts, the author presents a valuable treatise on food and drink, industry and commerce, warfare, religion, and so forth.

**382** *Biblical Archaeology Today.* 2 vols. Jerusalem: Israel Exploration Society, 1985–93.

These publications amount to proceedings from the first and second International Congresses on Biblical Archaeology held at Jerusalem in 1984 and 1990. Leading scholars address various aspects of archaeology related to the Scriptures.

**383** L. J. Hoppe. *What Are They Saying about Biblical Archaeology?* New York: Paulist, 1984.

With particular attention given to case-study sites of Ebla, Jerusalem, Capernaum, and Nabratein, the author summarizes the impact that archaeology has had on biblical understanding.

**384** H. Shanks and B. Mazar (eds.). *Recent Archaeology in the Land of Israel.* Translated by A. Finkelstein. Washington: Biblical Archaeology Society, 1984. Original title: *Thirty Years of Archaeology in Eretz-Israel* (in Hebrew). Jerusalem: Israel Exploration Society, 1978.

A series of essays by Israeli scholars on archaeological activity in Israel (including recent exploration at Jerusalem) makes up the contents of this book.

**385** E. M. Blaiklock and R. K. Harrison (eds.). *The New International Dictionary of Biblical Archaeology.* Grand Rapids: Zondervan, 1983.

This volume is quite helpful because of its over eight hundred individual articles about archaeological topics.

**386** R. E. Brown. *Recent Discoveries and the Biblical World.* Wilmington, Del.: Glazier, 1983.

This handy guide discusses around two dozen of the most significant finds made in our times and explains how they broaden our knowledge of the biblical world.

**387** H. F. Vos. *An Introduction to Bible Archaeology.* Rev. ed. Chicago: Moody, 1983.

In an easy to understand manner, this volume answers questions commonly asked about archaeology—such as how digs are conducted and how evidence is dated.

**388** Y. Aharoni. *The Archaeology of the Land of Israel.* Translated by A. F. Rainey. Philadelphia: Westminster/London: SCM, 1982. Original title: *Idem* (in Hebrew). Jerusalem: Shikmona, 1978.

The author discusses archaeological remains ranging from the palaeolithic through the First Temple period. Many figures and photos accompany the clearly written text.

**389** J. A. Thompson. *The Bible and Archaeology.* 3d ed. Grand Rapids: Eerdmans, 1982.

The writer brings together a concise summary (lavishly illustrated) of the information that is available for the study of the biblical records as a result of many years of excavation in Bible lands.

**390** *Biblical Archaeology Slide Set.* Washington: Biblical Archaeology Society, 1981.

Building materials, weapons, figurines, tombs, writing materials, and much more, are featured in 134 slides taken by world-renowned photographers. A detailed caption book gives information about both sites and artifacts.

**391** H. D. Lance. *The Old Testament and the Archaeologist.* Philadelphia: Fortress/London: SPCK, 1981.

The author explains the principles of excavation and how recovered materials are brought to bear on biblical studies, and he suggests practical ways for the beginner to track down needed information in the confusing array of primary and secondary publications.

**392** R. Moorey. *Excavation in Palestine.* Cities of the Biblical World. Grand Rapids: Eerdmans/Guildford, England: Lutterworth, 1981.

This illustrated, popular account of digging exploration in the Holy Land includes a description of archaeology's proper relationship to the Bible.

393  K. M. Kenyon. *Archaeology in the Holy Land*. 4th ed. New York: Norton/London: Benn, 1979. Reprinted Nashville: Nelson/London: Methuen, 1985.

This intellectually sound synthesis pays special attention to Jericho, Megiddo, and similar key sites.

394  M. S. Miller, J. L. Miller, B. M. Bennett, Jr., and D. H. Scott. *Harper's Encyclopedia of Bible Life*. Rev. ed. San Francisco: Harper, 1978.

Based on the latest finds, this illustrated publication on daily life in the biblical era acquaints readers more fully with a given period, event, or passage.

395  K. N. Schoville. *Biblical Archaeology in Focus*. Grand Rapids: Baker, 1978.

This significant title is divided into three parts: the first fosters an overall comprehension of biblical archaeology; the second surveys sites outside the Holy Land; the third records finds within Palestine.

396  K. A. Kitchen. *The Bible in Its World: The Bible and Archaeology Today*. Downers Grove, Ill.: Inter-Varsity/Exeter: Paternoster, 1977.

Concentrating principally upon the earlier periods of the Old Testament story (down to the end of Solomon's reign), this author studies pertinent ancient Near Eastern remains.

397  H. F. Vos. *Archaeology in Bible Lands*. Chicago: Moody, 1977.

The author introduces students to archaeological methodology, describes individual biblical sites that have been excavated, and supplies glossaries and bibliographies.

398  W. G. Dever. *Archaeology and Biblical Studies: Retrospects and Prospects*. Evanston: Seabury, 1974.

The author characterizes some contemporary trends among American archaeologists of the Holy Land and attempted to redefine appropriate relationships between biblical studies and Palestinian archaeology.

**399**  E. Yamauchi. *The Stones and the Scriptures.* Philadelphia: Lippincott, 1972. London: Inter-Varsity, 1973. Reprinted Grand Rapids: Baker, 1981.

   The author, who is committed to the historic Christian faith, seeks to summarize in selective fashion archaeological evidence and its bearings upon the Bible.

**400**  R. K. Harrison. *Old Testament Times.* Grand Rapids: Eerdmans, 1970.

   The writer draws from the cultures of Israel's surrounding nations in word and picture to provide a very helpful perspective on the Old Testament.

**401**  D. N. Freedman and J. C. Greenfield (eds.). *New Directions in Biblical Archaeology.* Garden City, N.Y.: Doubleday, 1969.

   This book collects reflections and research results from a symposium of leaders in the archaeological field; several articles on the Qumran manuscripts have been added.

**402**  P. W. Lapp. *Biblical Archaeology and History.* New York: World, 1969.

   Aiming to communicate with undergraduates and not to converse with colleagues, the writer explores connections between the Bible (on the one hand) and archaeology and history (on the other).

**403**  Archaeological Institute of America. *Archaeological Discoveries in the Holy Land.* New York: Bonanza, 1967.

   This volume records activity in Palestine during approximately two decades following World War II. The writers for most of the book's chapters were the excavators themselves.

**404**  D. W. Thomas (ed.). *Archaeology and Old Testament Study.* Oxford: Clarendon, 1967.

   A lengthy Scripture index succeeds an extensive review of the actual literary and historical sources of the ancient world from which archaeological information comes.

**405**  W. G. Williams. *Archaeology in Biblical Research.* New York: Abingdon, 1965. London: Lutterworth, 1966.

In addition to aims and aspects of archaeology, the author outlines the fruit of archaeology—what it has taught us about the world of the Bible.

**406** H. J. Franken and C. A. Franken-Battershill. *A Primer of Old Testament Archaeology*. Leiden: Brill, 1963.

Written mainly for theological students, this manual intends to put into their hands necessary tools for extracting relevant information from excavation reports—information that has a direct bearing on the task of interpreting the Bible.

**407** J. Gray. *Archaeology and the Old Testament World*. New York: Harper/London: Nelson, 1962.

The writer conducts the reader through the "museum" of the ancient Near East in order to present the world where the Israelites encountered their problems and sought to solve them.

**408** G. E. Wright. *Biblical Archaeology*. New ed. Philadelphia: Westminster/London: Duckworth, 1962.

In an arresting manner this reliable work locates the biblical narrative within the context of archaeological discovery. The material is arranged in historical sequence from prehistoric times to the New Testament period.

**409** R. de Vaux. *Ancient Israel: Its Life and Institutions*. Translated by J. McHugh. New York: McGraw/London: Darton, 1961. Original title: *Les institutions de l'Ancien Testament*. Paris: Cerf, 1961–67.

Written for the nonspecialist by a scholar who lived in Palestine for many years, this indispensable handbook studies topics like nomadism, religion, the family, government, and the military as reflected in the Old Testament, ancient history, and archaeology.

**410** W. F. Albright. *The Archaeology of Palestine*. Rev. ed. Harmondsworth, England: Penguin, 1960. Reprinted Gloucester, Mass.: Smith, 1971.

This valuable, erudite survey reports on archaeological accomplishments at ancient Palestinian sites. The author devotes the final third of the book to peoples, languages, writing, daily life, and so on.

**411** W. Corswant. *A Dictionary of Life in Bible Times*. Translated by A. W. Heathcote. New York: Oxford University/London: Hodder, 1960. Original title: *Dictionnaire d'archéologie biblique*. Neuchâtel: Delachaux, 1956.

Supported by illustrations and scriptural references, entries cover in detail the personal, social, and religious life of the ancient Israelites and early Christians.

**412** J. B. Pritchard. *Archaeology and the Old Testament*. Princeton: Princeton University, 1958.

In nontechnical language that the layperson can comprehend, the author assesses the kind of change that archaeology has brought about since the midnineteenth century in viewing the biblical past.

**413** E. W. Heaton. *Everyday Life in Old Testament Times*. New York: Scribner's/London: Batsford, 1956. Reprinted London: Transworld, 1974.

This illustrated study of material pertinent to culture and society in Old Testament times aids students in understanding the total setting of the Scriptures.

**414** Studies in Biblical Archaeology. 9 vols. London: SCM, 1955–58.

Written with enthusiasm and abounding in illustrations, these commendable volumes acquaint the layperson with various results of scholarly archaeological research.

## 5.2 Geography

This section includes atlases of the Promised Land in addition to books on the historical geography of those lands. Discussions about such matters as plants, roads, and animals are also found here.

**415** Y. Aharoni, M. Avi-Yonah, A. F. Rainey, and Z. Safrai. *The Macmillan Bible Atlas*. 3d ed. New York: Macmillan, 1993.

Maps and text depict religious, political, military, and economic events of the Old Testament, Second Temple, Intertestamental, New Testament, and Early Church eras in biblical history.

**416**  F. N. Hepper. *Baker Encyclopedia of Bible Plants*. Grand Rapids: Baker, 1993. British edition: *Illustrated Encyclopedia of Bible Plants*. Leicester: Inter-Varsity, 1992.

This is a botanically authoritative reference guide to all that grows in Bible lands. Full-color photographs and exacting drawings illustrate the text throughout.

**417**  C. R. Page II and C. A. Volz. *The Land and the Book: An Introduction to the World of the Bible*. Nashville: Abingdon, 1993.

In this fascinating exploration of history, culture, and geography, the authors briefly describe each of the major areas in which events of the biblical narrative took place.

**418**  D. A. Dorsey. *The Roads and Highways of Ancient Israel*. ASOR Library of Biblical and Near Eastern Archaeology. Baltimore: Johns Hopkins University, 1991.

A discussion of Hebrew road terminology in the Old Testament supplements a detailed treatment of the author's reconstruction of ancient Israel's road network.

**419**  J. B. Pritchard (ed.). *The Harper Concise Atlas of the Bible*. New York: Harper, 1991.

Illustrated with hundreds of maps, site reconstructions, and color photographs, this accessible edition conveys an almost tangible sense of biblical lands, events, and peoples.

**420**  H. T. Frank (ed.). *Atlas of the Bible Lands*. Rev. ed. Maplewood, N.J.: Hammond, 1990.

The editor helps students of Scripture understand the setting of biblical history through fresh maps, evocative photographs, graphic city plans, and time charts.

**421**  C. G. Rasmussen. *NIV Atlas of the Bible*. Grand Rapids: Zondervan, 1989.

The author does an excellent job of clearly and succinctly surveying the geography as well as the history of the Promised Land and ancient Near East.

**422**  J. C. Laney. *Baker's Concise Bible Atlas: A Geographical Survey of Bible History*. Grand Rapids: Baker, 1988.

Since one cannot totally comprehend biblical history apart from its physical setting, this book explains and illustrates the historical role of geography.

**423** D. Baly. *Basic Biblical Geography*. Philadelphia: Fortress, 1987.

The author, a trained geographer who lived in the Middle East for many years, presents a concise yet comprehensive overview of the geography of ancient Palestine.

**424** J. B. Pritchard. *The Harper Atlas of the Bible*. New York: Harper/Toronto: Fitzhenry, 1987. British edition: *The Times Atlas of the Bible*. London: Times, 1987.

With a wealth of interesting information presented in a graphically compelling way, this technical atlas covers the period of time from before biblical events to the founding of Byzantine churches.

**425** Z. Kallai. *Historical Geography of the Bible: The Tribal Territories of Israel*. Leiden: Brill/Jerusalem: Magnes, 1986. Original title: *The Allotments of the Tribes of Israel* (in Hebrew). Jerusalem: Bialik, 1967.

The writer geographically and historically analyzes and describes the tribal boundary system of early Israel. This book includes extensive tables, indexes, and maps.

**426** *Atlas of Israel: Cartography, Physical and Human Geography*. 3d ed. New York: Macmillan, 1985.

Although this excellent atlas is primarily intended as a tool for the study of modern Israel, it has numerous maps pertinent to the periods of the Old Testament.

**427** B. J. Beitzel. *The Moody Atlas of Bible Lands*. Chicago: Moody, 1985.

The author uses a combination of impressive photographs, superior maps, and well-written prose to describe physically and historically the Promised Land and the surrounding territories.

**428** J. Rogerson. *Atlas of the Bible*. New York: Facts on File, 1985. British edition: *The New Atlas of the Bible*. London: Macdonald, 1985. Reprinted Oxford: Phaidon, 1989.

The amount of attention the writer gives to geography as opposed to history in this fine volume supplies users with a superb feel for the different regions of Israel.

**429** D. R. W. Wood (ed.). *New Bible Atlas*. Wheaton: Tyndale/ Leicester: Inter-Varsity, 1985.

This highly competent, brief atlas (which covers the Old and New Testaments) has a helpful section that treats lands outside Israel.

**430** H. G. May (ed.). *Oxford Bible Atlas*. Revised by J. Day. 3d ed. Oxford: Oxford University, 1984.

This compact but outstanding atlas features well-done, easy-to-read maps and an extensive gazetteer, together with a summary of history from the patriarchs to Paul.

**431** *Eerdmans' Atlas of the Bible with A-Z Guide to Places*. Grand Rapids: Eerdmans, 1983.

This compact guide—with full-color maps, charts, and photographs as well as an easy-to-read text—helps readers understand the geographical and historical context of significant scriptural events.

**432** F. F. Bruce. *Bible History Atlas*. New York: Crossroad/Jerusalem: Carta, 1982.

With content (text and maps) designed for the beginner, this work very simply traces events in biblical history from the Creation to the Jewish revolt against the Romans in A.D. 132.

**433** M. Zohary. *Plants of the Bible*. London: Cambridge University, 1982.

Prepared by one of Israel's foremost botanists, this complete handbook to all the plants of the Bible includes color plates, a glossary, and a Scripture-reference index.

**434** J. L. Gardner (ed.). *Reader's Digest Atlas of the Bible: An Illustrated Guide to the Holy Land*. Pleasantville, N.Y.: Reader's Digest, 1981.

Multicolor maps, illustrations, photographs, reproductions, and reconstructions supplement the descriptive copy as well as a gazetteer of scriptural place names.

**435**  Y. Aharoni. *The Land of the Bible: A Historical Geography.*
Edited by A. F. Rainey. Rev. ed. Philadelphia: Westminster/
London: Burns, 1979.

This fine, authoritative study on Holy Land geography
(weather, agriculture, topography, and the like) describes
Palestine throughout the ages, stopping with the Persian
period.

**436**  C. F. Pfeiffer. *Baker's Bible Atlas.* Rev. ed. Grand Rapids:
Baker, 1979.

Accompanied by photographs as well as both colored and
black-and-white maps, the text follows the scriptural narrative from Genesis through Revelation.

**437**  *Student Map Manual: Historical Geography of the Bible
Lands.* Jerusalem: Pictorical Archive, 1979.

This unique and innovative atlas of Palestine has regional, archaeological, and historical maps with eastern
orientation and horizontal format rather than northern
and vertical.

**438**  M. Avi-Yonah. *The Holy Land from the Persian to the Arab
Conquests (536 B.C. to A.D. 640).* Rev. ed. Baker Studies in
Biblical Archaeology. Grand Rapids: Baker, 1977. Original
title: *A Historical Geography of the Land of Israel* (in Hebrew). Jerusalem: Bialik, 1984.

Serving almost as a sequel to the geography by Aharoni
(#435), this work discusses—but in less detail—the land
of Palestine according to various periods from the Persian
to the Arabian.

**439**  E. M. Blaiklock (ed.). *The Zondervan Pictorial Bible Atlas.*
Grand Rapids: Zondervan, 1972.

This worthwhile book features both full-color and one-
color maps accompanying text on the history, geography,
climate, and other characteristics of the area.

**440**  D. Baly and A. D. Tushingham. *Atlas of the Biblical World.*
New York: World, 1971.

A major goal of this work, which emphasizes physical
and human geography, was to assist users in visualizing
the Palestinian environment within its Middle Eastern
framework.

**441** G. Cansdale. *All the Animals of the Bible Lands*. Grand Rapids: Zondervan, 1970. British edition: *Animals of Bible Lands*. Exeter: Paternoster, 1970.

> The writer explains the region's topography, geology, and climate before describing every beast, bird, and fish (plus more) in the Old and New Testaments.

**442** G. Bare. *Plants and Animals of the Bible: A Translators' Workbook*. London: United Bible Societies, 1969.

> All terms in this compilation are transliterated and briefly defined, with scientific equivalents noted when ascertainable. Biblical references are also supplied.

**443** J. H. Negenman. *New Atlas of the Bible*. Translated by H. Hoskins and R. Beckley. Garden City, N.Y.: Doubleday/ London: Collins, 1969. Original title: *De bakermat van de Bijbel*. Amsterdam: Elsevier, 1968.

> Superb and abundant illustrations enable readers to picture the culture and achievement of the peoples of the world in which the Bible was born.

**444** C. F. Pfeiffer and H. F. Vos. *The Wycliffe Historical Geography of Bible Lands*. Chicago: Moody, 1967.

> The writers have sought to bring together geographical, historical, and archaeological data on the "biblical" areas of the Near Eastern and Mediterranean world.

**445** D. Baly. *Geographical Companion to the Bible*. New York: McGraw/London: Lutterworth/Toronto: Ryerson, 1963.

> The writer stresses those factors (such as the main trade routes and the natural battlefields) that helped determine the ways of life for people in biblical times.

**446** H. H. Rowley. *The Teach Yourself Bible Atlas*. London: English Universities, 1960. Reprinted *The Modern Reader's Bible Atlas*. New York: Association, 1961.

> Colored maps (followed by a gazetteer), clear text (on geography as well as history and even archaeology), and numerous plates (showing what scriptural places look like) constitute this book.

**447** L. H. Grollenberg. *Shorter Atlas of the Bible*. Translated by M. F. Hedlund. Edinburgh: Nelson, 1959. Reprinted *The*

*Penguin Shorter Atlas of the Bible.* Harmondsworth, England: Penguin, 1978. Original title: *Kleine atlas van de Bijbel.* Amsterdam: Elsevier, 1959.

> This combination of maps, photographs, and text is an attempt to present in small compass a picture of the world in which the books of the Bible found their origin.

**448** J. Simons. *The Geographical and Topographical Texts of the Old Testament.* Studia Francisci Scholten Memoriae Dicata 2. Leiden: Brill, 1959.

> For both students and scholars, the author interprets the Old Testament's geographical texts and identifies every place name mentioned from Genesis to Maccabees.

**449** L. H. Grollenberg. *Atlas of the Bible.* Translated by J. M. H. Reid and H. H. Rowley. London: Nelson, 1956. Original title: *Atlas van de Bijbel.* Amsterdam: Elsevier, 1954.

> This highly recommendable atlas blends history and topography. An ingenious use of symbols on the maps incorporates a great deal of information.

**450** E. G. Kraeling. *Rand McNally Bible Atlas.* Chicago: Rand, 1956.

> In a work intended principally for advanced students, the writer reliably details and discusses geographic and topographic references from Genesis to Revelation.

**451** G. E. Wright and F. V. Filson. *The Westminster Historical Atlas to the Bible.* Rev. ed. Westminster Aids to the Study of the Scriptures. Philadelphia: Westminster, 1956.

> A series of maps vividly sets forth the geographical setting of the Scriptures; explanatory chapters provide essential facts needed to comprehend it.

**452** G. A. Smith. *The Historical Geography of the Holy Land.* 4th ed. London: Hodder, 1896. Reprinted Jerusalem: Ariel, 1974.

> Though now outmoded in much of its detail, this graphic description of the historical geography of Palestine has remained a classic over the years.

## 5.3 History

These volumes concentrate on the history of ancient Israel. Some handle the broad sweep of that history; others select portions of shorter duration. The so-called "intertestamental" period is not slighted. Works outlining chronology or explaining historiography appear in noticeable number.

**453**  A. R. Millard, J. K. Hoffmeier, and D. W. Baker (eds.). *Faith, Tradition, and History: Old Testament Historiography in Its Near Eastern Context.* Winona Lake, Ind.: Eisenbrauns, 1994.

These papers explore some of the ways that the ancient Hebrew writers and their contemporaries presented history and how their work should be understood today.

**454**  G. W. Ahlström. *The History of Ancient Palestine.* Edited by D. Edelman. Minneapolis: Fortress/Sheffield: JSOT, 1993.

Considering all available source material—textual, epigraphic, and archaeological—the writer creatively presents the history from the earliest times to Alexander's conquest of the Near East.

**455**  J. A. Soggin. *An Introduction to the History of Israel and Judah.* Valley Forge: Trinity/London: SCM, 1993.

A complete revision of the author's earlier work, this standard book addresses all aspects of Hebrew history and historiography—politics, economics, religion, theology, methodology, geography, and topography.

**456**  J. Pixley. *Biblical Israel: A People's History.* Minneapolis: Fortress, 1992. Original title: *Historia sagrada, historia popular.* San Jose, Costa Rica: DEI, 1991.

The author deftly sketches Jewish history from the nation's presumed origins in peasant uprisings of the fourteenth century B.C. to the uprising of the second century A.D.

**457**  H. Shanks (ed.). *The Rise of Ancient Israel.* Washington: Biblical Archaeology Society, 1992.

Written for the layperson, this volume is an up-to-date and understandable discussion of the key archaeological, historical, and literary issues associated with the emergence of Israel.

**458**  K. A. D. Smelik. *Converting the Past: Studies in Ancient Israelite and Moabite Historiography.* Oudtestamentische Studiën 28. Leiden: Brill, 1992.

All of the chapters in this volume are connected in one way or another with problems related to the use of texts from the Hebrew Bible for historical research.

**459**  T. L. Thompson. *Early History of the Israelite People.* Studies in the History of the Ancient Near East 4. Leiden: Brill, 1992.

This book surrounds a description of early Israel with many historiographical considerations and discusses economic processes impacting on the nation's development.

**460**  W. H. Barnes. *Studies in the Chronology of the Divided Monarchy of Israel.* Harvard Semitic Monographs 48. Atlanta: Scholars, 1991.

In order to formulate a tentative but reasonable chronology of Hebrew kings, the author grapples with various chronographic data from several contemporary civilizations of the ancient Near East.

**461**  D. V. Edelman (ed.). *The Fabric of History: Text, Artifact, and Israel's Past.* JSOTSup 127. Sheffield: JSOT, 1991.

The focus of the six essays gathered here is very much on methodology in the reconstruction of history. There is an index of biblical references.

**462**  R. B. Coote. *Early Israel: A New Horizon.* Minneapolis: Fortress, 1990.

The author is both original and provocative in this state-of-the-art, accessible introduction to the basic historical elements of Israel's emergence.

**463**  D. F. Hinson. *History of Israel.* Rev. ed. TEF Study Guide 7. Vol. 1 of *Old Testament Introduction.* London: SPCK, 1990.

Drawing on the latest findings by biblicists and archaeologists, this fascinating account of the history of the Jews includes maps, topical photographs, and study suggestions.

**464** R. L. Cate. *A History of the Bible Lands in the Interbiblical Period*. Nashville: Broadman, 1989.

Communicating the results of research in lucid prose, the writer introduces the reader to the era's people, geography, politics, religions, philosophies, and lifestyles.

**465** J. H. Hayes and P. K. Hooker. *A New Chronology for the Kings of Israel and Judah and Its Implications for Biblical History and Literature*. Atlanta: Knox, 1988.

Utilizing all available and reliable evidence, the authors establish not only regnal years for the Hebrew rulers but also specific dates for numerous events in Israelite and Judaean history.

**466** N. P. Lemche. *Ancient Israel: A New History of Israelite Society*. The Biblical Seminar 5. Sheffield: JSOT, 1988. Original title: *Det gamle Israel*. Arhus: Anis, 1984.

In this provocative text, the writer presents a new model for how we should understand Israelite history—a reconstruction from archaeological results, nonbiblical evidence, and the Old Testament.

**467** H. Shanks (ed.). *Ancient Israel: A Short History from Abraham to the Roman Destruction of the Temple*. Washington: Biblical Archaeology Society, 1988. London: SPCK, 1989.

Prominent Jewish and Christian scholars have contributed pieces reflecting recently developed perspectives. The book exhibits over forty full-color and black-and-white pictures.

**468** R. B. Coote and K. W. Whitelam. *The Emergence of Early Israel in Historical Perspective*. The Social World of Biblical Antiquity Series 5. Sheffield: Almond, 1987.

This study moves from a broad treatment of the issues of historiography and Palestinian history to a more focused discussion of the emergence and transformation of early Israel.

**469** E. H. Merrill. *Kingdom of Priests: A History of Old Testament Israel*. Grand Rapids: Baker, 1987.

This book approaches the history as an integration of political, social, economic, and religious factors on the basis of Scripture, archaeology, and extrabiblical literature.

**470** J. M. Miller and J. H. Hayes. *A History of Ancient Israel and Judah.* Philadelphia: Westminster/London: SCM, 1986.

The incorporation of significant ancient documents, maps, charts, and photographs enhance the new and convincing reconstruction of Hebrew history in this textbook for undergraduates.

**471** L. J. Wood. *A Survey of Israel's History.* Revised by D. O'Brien. Grand Rapids: Zondervan, 1986.

This book, which includes a chapter on the intertestamental period, is geared for the college classroom and essentially retells the biblical story with added archaeological information.

**472** F. Castel. *The History of Israel and Judah in Old Testament Times.* Translated by M. J. O'Connell. New York: Paulist, 1985. Original title: *L'histoire d'Israel et de Juda.* Paris: Centurion, 1983.

Maps, charts, and drawings help make the major moments of Old Testament history come alive for the ordinary reader and student in this careful and balanced treatment.

**473** R. L. Cate. *These Sought a Country: A History of Israel in Old Testament Times.* Nashville: Broadman, 1985.

Each chapter includes sources for study and problems for consideration, and discusses major events along with their significance. The book contains maps of different periods.

**474** H. Jagersma. *A History of Israel from Alexander the Great to Bar Kochba.* London: SCM, 1985/Philadelphia: Fortress, 1986. Original title: *Geschiedenis van Israël van Alexander de Grote tot Bar Kochba.* Kampen, Netherlands: Kok, 1985.

A sequel to his previous work (#481), this book continues the history of the Jews up to A.D. 135. Bibliographical references permit more detailed study of summary statements.

**475** N. P. Lemche. *Early Israel: Anthropological and Historical Studies on the Israelite Society before the Monarchy.* Supplements to Vetus Testamentum 37. Leiden: Brill, 1985.

With prudence and vigor, the author has analyzed the three main theories regarding Israel's origins and has contributed greatly to the ongoing discussion of those theories.

**476** M. Grant. *The History of Ancient Israel.* New York: Scribner's/London: Weidenfeld, 1984.

This account of ancient Israel, extending from its beginnings to the destruction of Jerusalem and the Temple in A.D. 70, is based as objectively as possible on excavations and Scripture.

**477** D. N. Freedman and D. F. Graf (eds.). *Palestine in Transition: The Emergence of Ancient Israel.* The Social World of Biblical Antiquity Series 2. Sheffield: Almond, 1983.

This collection of essays deals with models or hypotheses put forth to explain how the Hebrews gained control over the land of Canaan.

**478** B. Halpern. *The Emergence of Israel in Canaan.* Society of Biblical Literature Monograph Series 29. Chico, Calif.: Scholars, 1983.

This promising approach to the subject of premonarchic Israel opens up new vistas by taking as its point of departure the temporal framework of the period.

**479** E. R. Thiele. *The Mysterious Numbers of the Hebrew Kings.* 3d ed. Grand Rapids: Zondervan, 1983.

Providing analytical argumentation and ingenious solutions, the author handles the difficult problem of synchronizing the scriptural chronologies of the Israelite and Judahite monarchs.

**480** J. Van Seters. *In Search of History: Historiography in the Ancient World and the Origins of Biblical History.* New Haven: Yale University, 1983.

Before expanding on Israelite or biblical historiography, the writer examines ancient Greek, Mesopotamian, Hittite, Egyptian, and Syro-Palestinian historiographies for perspective.

**481** H. Jagersma. *A History of Israel in the Old Testament Period.* Translated by J. Bowden. London: SCM, 1982/Philadelphia: Fortress, 1983. Original title: *Geschiedenis van Israël in het oudtestamentische tijdvak*. Kampen, Netherlands: Kok, 1979.

> With comparative brevity and simplicity, the writer states clearly at every stage the problems in recounting Israel's history and the evidence available for solving them.

**482** J. J. Bimson. *Redating the Exodus and Conquest*. 2d ed. JSOTSup 5. Sheffield: Almond, 1981.

> This book seeks to unravel a tangled web of evidence and argument concerning the dates of these two great events of biblical history.

**483** J. Bright. *A History of Israel*. 3d ed. Philadelphia: Westminster/London: SCM, 1981.

> This systematic presentation is cautious, judicious, and thorough. It has good maps and excellent chronological charts, and it integrates material from Near Eastern archaeological investigations.

**484** S. Herrmann. *A History of Israel in Old Testament Times*. Translated by J. Bowden. 2d ed. Philadelphia: Fortress/London: SCM, 1981. Original title: *Geschichte Israels in alttestamentlicher Zeit*. Munich: Kaiser, 1980.

> This very readable and useful survey was written as an introductory manual for students. The book covers the periods of Israel's history down to 63 B.C.

**485** J. J. Davis and J. C. Whitcomb. *A History of Israel*. Grand Rapids: Baker, 1980.

> Describing the history of Israel principally for the laity, this volume follows the biblical story line closely and interpolates archaeological facts where pertinent.

**486** R. de Vaux. *The Early History of Israel*. Translated by D. Smith. Philadelphia: Westminster/London: Darton, 1978. Original title: *Histoire ancienne d'Israël*. Paris: Gabalda, 1971–73.

> Interrupted unfortunately by the author's death, this masterful work still treats the history comprehensively from Israel's beginnings up to the period of the judges.

**487** J. H. Hayes and J. M. Miller (eds.). *Israelite and Judaean History*. Philadelphia: Westminster/London: SCM, 1977. Reprinted Philadelphia: Trinity, 1990.

The fourteen contributors of international repute treat specific periods of history—from the patriarchal to the Roman. An appendix supplies a chronology of Hebrew monarchs.

**488** J. M. Miller. *The Old Testament and the Historian*. Philadelphia: Fortress/London: SPCK, 1976.

Explaining for beginning student and mature scholar how historians go about their work, the author illustrates difficulties involved in relating archaeological data to the testimony of written sources.

**489** B. K. Rattey. *A Short History of the Hebrews from the Patriarchs to Herod the Great*. Revised by P. M. Binyon. 3d ed. London: Oxford University, 1976.

Consideration of the many different sources of historical material precedes the history proper. Each chapter ends with suggestions to help students in studying this textbook.

**490** G. Larsson. *The Secret System: A Study in the Chronology of the Old Testament*. Leiden: Brill, 1973.

Written not only for the scholar, this book concludes that the Old Testament's chronological system was deliberately obscured by those who designed it.

**491** C. F. Pfeiffer. *Old Testament History*. Grand Rapids: Baker, 1973.

This helpful history of Israel draws on a wide variety of archaeological finds while following very closely the biblical subject matter and sequence of events.

**492** P. Ackroyd. *Exile and Restoration: A Study of Hebrew Thought of the Sixth Century B.C.* Philadelphia: Westminster/London: SCM, 1968.

This classic study covers the sixth century B.C., when the Jews were in Babylonian captivity. The book also narrates their return and reconstruction after Persia conquered Babylon.

**493**  *The World History of the Jewish People.* New Brunswick: Rutgers University, 1964– .

> The first series of very thorough volumes in this multiauthor set deals with ancient times, from the dawn of civilization through the second temple period.

**494**  W. F. Albright. *The Biblical Period from Abraham to Ezra.* New York: Harper, 1963.

> This short account, which traces the history of Israel in broad outlines, is nonetheless packed with information and has had much influence.

**495**  F. F. Bruce. *Israel and the Nations.* Grand Rapids: Eerdmans, 1963. Reprinted Exeter: Paternoster, 1973.

> This unusual book, which combines research and interpretation with readability, recounts the story of ancient Israel from the Exodus to the fall of Jerusalem in A.D. 70.

**496**  E. J. Bickerman. *From Ezra to the Last of the Maccabees: Foundations of Post-Biblical Judaism.* New York: Schocken, 1962.

> The author examines the elements that shaped the Jewish people after their return from Babylonian exile and transformed them into a major historical force.

**497**  E. L. Ehrlich. *A Concise History of Israel from the Earliest Times to the Destruction of the Temple in A.D. 70.* Translated by J. Barr. New York: Harper/London: Darton, 1962. Original title: *Geschichte Israels.* Berlin: de Gruyter, 1958.

> Using archaeological exploration and research, this well-documented and worthy volume for serious students illuminates the biblical record beginning with the Patriarchs.

**498**  M. Noth. *The History of Israel.* Translated by P. R. Ackroyd. 2d ed. New York: Harper/London: Black, 1960. Reprinted London: SCM, 1983. Original title: *Geschichte Israels.* Göttingen: Vandenhoeck, 1954.

> This classic formulation of Israelite history is full of erudition and insight. The treatment extends from the tribal origins of the Hebrews up to the Roman era.

**499** H. M. Orlinsky. *Ancient Israel.* 2d ed. The Development of Western Civilization. Ithaca: Cornell University, 1960. Reprinted Westport, Conn.: Greenwood, 1981.

This lively essay provides a brief narrative account of the history of those who created the Hebrew Bible. The volume includes suggestions for further reading.

**500** J. Bright. *Early Israel in Recent History Writing: A Study in Method.* Studies in Biblical Theology 19. Chicago: Allenson/London: SCM, 1956.

After an exposition and critique of certain historiographical approaches of the day, the author sketches his preferred method for writing the early history of Israel.

# Index of Authors